Why Do I Fill My Li
Wonder Why I Feel

A companion guide for individuals in therapy for depression and anxiety

D. Rachel Coleman

Copyright 2016

ISBN-13: 978-1523413522
ISBN-10: 1523413522

©Why Do I Fill My Life with Mess Then Wonder Why I Feel like Crap ™

A companion guide for individuals in therapy for depression and anxiety

All rights reserved.

No part of this book may be reproduced in any form or by any electronic or mechanical means, including information storage and retrieval systems, without the express written permission of the author.

Disclaimer: This book is not a substitute for professional medical or psychological advice.

To my first love my husband John, our four children Krissia, Raina, Mina, and Emerson, and our grandchildren Christian and Karter. You all are my world.

Change is scary no matter how many times we manage it. In our minds we make doing something different or new harder than it actually is. Once we attain success, often we exclaim, "I should have done it sooner!" and we sour the accomplishment by beating ourselves up for wasting so much time being stuck.

Some of this madness is human nature, but most of it is rooted in the fear of the unknown, complacency, and even laziness. An insane person does not choose to be insane; however, many of us choose to be unhappy. Who, then, is truly insane?

One of the hardest lessons in life is letting go. Whether it's guilt, anger, love, loss or betrayal. Change is never easy. We fight to hold on, and we fight to let go. –Rawforbeauty.com

Table of Contents

Preface	1
Introduction	2
Chapter One – In Search of Happiness	
Why I wrote this book	4
What does happiness mean to you?	7
You are not alone	10
Chapter Two – Treatment Information	
What is cognitive behavioral therapy & Solution focused therapy?	11
What level of therapy is best for you?	14
Ten tips to get more out of therapy	17
Chapter Three – Depression & Anxiety 101	
How depression and anxiety feed each other	24
Depression FYI	25
Anxiety FYI	27
Chapter Four – What I Have Seen	
My observations of situational depression and anxiety	29
Chapter Five – Let's Get Started	
Healing through examples	33
Anxiety	36
Stressed and overwhelmed	51
Low self-esteem	69
Family problems	90
Health issues	105
Addiction	115
Relationships	122
Sexual Assault	141
Chapter Six - Something to think about	
Changing your mental mindset	158
Everyone has the capacity to change their life	160

      Don't let someone else's mess affect your happiness   162
      Deal with reality   166
Conclusion   170
References   173

PREFACE

Human behavior has always fascinated me. I remember as a young child being scolded for observing and listening to every word that rolled off the tongue of the older folk as they conversed in the kitchen. Many times my mother's sister looked down at me and reprimanded me to "get out of grown folk business" and to "go outside and play somewhere." This was followed by, "She always in grown folk business." Warily, I walked away, thinking what was being discussed at the kitchen table was far more interesting than what was going on outside.

Trying to make sense of why people do what they do has intrigued me since I was a little child. Today, I am particularly puzzled at why people hold on to painful emotional and psychological situations and turn them into agony when they have the capacity to end their suffering. How is it that one can say, "I want to get better," but do absolutely nothing to move toward that desire and remain clueless as to why they are in agony, suffering, and stagnation? Why is it that bad things can happen to one person and they overcome their plight, while others are devastated for the rest of their days?

INTRODUCTION

You rant and rave, "I want to be happy," but very little or nothing in your life reflects happiness. It's routine, rat race, and rut. You blame your mate or lack of a mate, your kids, your job, your past, and even God as the source of your unhappiness. The source of your unhappiness is you.

No one came out of his mother's womb and said, "I wanna be unhappy, depressed, and anxious when I grow up." You allowed life, someone, or a situation to steal your happiness and peace, or maybe you learned to believe that happiness was for others and not for you. Rather than do something about it, you decided to take the easy way and point the finger at everyone but yourself, keeping you in a cyclone of sadness, hopelessness, disappointment, and despair.

Some of us proclaim to others we're happy and put on a façade of happiness, while living a secret life of inner suffering. Daily some of us lie to ourselves and others and mask sadness and suffering with half-hearted smiles, material possessions, or resort to alcohol or drugs – legal and illegal – to give the illusion that we are happy. The need for excessive attention, being loud, ostentatious, bragging, belittling and being hypercritical of others, and sexual promiscuity can be signs of working double time to give the appearance that everything is okay when, in fact, the person is unhappy.

Even though I know better, every now and then I still get caught up trying to make it through this thing called life, and I may slip up and allow my happiness and peace to be stolen. However, I learned not to stay in this place too long and to regroup and get back on track quickly. When you stay in negative emotions too long, you can go mad.

Fortunately, we are all blessed with the ability to make choices in our lives. You can choose to live a happy, peaceful life or a mess-filled life of stress, strife, and struggle. Living a peaceful life is not complicated; it's really simple. It is easy once you decide to eliminate the mess from your life, change your mindset, and make wise choices. This does not mean that life will not have its ups and downs.

Unfortunately, so many of us have made the choice to keep our eye focused on the mess like fear, doubt, jealously, greed, gossip, lack, backstabbing, strife, struggle, discontent, unhappiness, and negative thoughts. Focusing on these things will only feed depression and anxiety and will never result in happiness.

I believe in God. If you don't, that's okay. Deep in my heart, I do not believe that God intended for anyone to live a life of suffering and misery. I also believe we cause most of our own unhappiness. Happiness is available to all – and not just a good moment here and there. I mean everlasting happiness and peace. With happiness and peace, life becomes so much easier and lighter. Little miracles start to happen. Doors open that you did not know existed, and struggles seem to fade away. Solutions to problems you've battled for years become crystal clear. You, too, can have this life. I suggest you at least give it a try.

CHAPTER ONE - IN SEARCH OF HAPPINESS
WHY I WROTE THIS BOOK

Namaste. I hope this book finds you well on your journey to healing. Realize that imperfect progress is progress. We are all works in progress, blessed with the ability to write, rewrite, and give richness, direction, and meaning to our everyday lives. The perfect person has yet to exist. Accept who you are, where you are, and the progress you make, however small.

It gives me great joy to put together this book. Writing this book contributes to fulfilling my sense of purpose and passion for assisting individuals to live healthy, happy, peaceful lives. There is no greater feeling for me than helping people transcend difficult situations. Frequently, I have been told by friends and family that my job is depressing. Yes, my vocation can be draining, and at times I have felt I was one episode away from the psychiatric unit myself. But my profession has also given me a great appreciation for life and physical and mental health that I probably would not have if I had not taken this particular path.

Usually I am interacting with people when they're at their lowest point or when they are going through some difficult situation. People are either suicidal, homicidal, or psychotic; have some type of mental- or physical-illness crisis; have experienced loss; or are on their way to glory. Dealing with death and sickness on a daily basis is just part of the job. Choosing to focus on maintaining my happiness and peace has enabled me to weather many circumstances and storms in my personal and professional life.

Many times I have tried to turn away from writing this book. Repeatedly, clients expressed that they needed something to keep them focused between sessions. It is the intent of this book to be that *something*. It is my intention for this book to expand on the discussions and the awareness gained during face-to-face therapy sessions. I have seen too many clients leave my office pumped up with new insight and awareness, only to retreat to their same old unproductive habits, behaviors, and responses once they reencounter their demons in the real world.

The goal of therapy is to empower, give us insight into ourselves, teach us to resolve issues in a healthy manner, offer new ways of thinking, and learn more productive ways to respond to life's ups and downs. The goal of therapy is not to become dependent on the therapist. I never respond to the frequent question clients ask, "What would you do?" It is in the best interest of clients to learn to think for themselves. I take this stance because, if what I tell you to do works, that's great. However, if what I tell you to do does not work, you will smear my name to anyone who will listen. Therefore, it is my goal to be encouraging and supportive as I teach clients how to problem-solve on their own.

The last thing any depressed or anxious person wants to do is read a thick, complicated book, so you will not find convoluted theories or pretentious language in this one. It is written concisely, using frank and straightforward, easy-to-understand language. This book contains practical tools for everyday people to put into their arsenal in order to discover and maintain happiness and live a life free of depression and anxiety.

To the naysayers: Yes, it is possible to live a life free of depression and anxiety. If you still need convincing of this, you may not find this book helpful. It is geared toward those who have already made the decision and are seriously committed to learning how to live a happy life.

My disclaimer: I must remind readers that this book offers information on situational depression and anxiety for individuals who desire to take charge of their lives and take the necessary steps toward living a happy, more fulfilling life. **Medically, organically, or biologically rooted depression and anxiety are beyond the scope of this book and require more intensive treatment.** Further, this book is not intended to be a substitute for actual therapy or treatment.

WHAT DOES HAPPINESS MEAN TO YOU?

If you fell in a pile of shit, would you just sit there? Would you just sit there and sigh and contemplate how hard it is to get out of it? As you catch the gazes of passersby would you loudly profess that you wished to get out of the pile of shit? As the pile got funkier and the stench gets worse, would you think, "If only someone would help get me out of this shit?" Perhaps while festering in this crap, you would rant about how unfair it is that you fell in the pile of shit in the first place. Surely blaming and pointing fingers would get you out.

An absurd line of thinking? Maybe, but this is exactly what a lot of individuals do when experiencing situational depression and anxiety. They set up camp with depression and anxiety and bemoan how hard it is to get out of it. The words *wish* and *if only* are used a lot. A great number expect someone or something to rescue them or are waiting for "the right." They are waiting for the right partner, the right job, the right money, or the right pill before they will make a move. Meanwhile, life is just passing by.

Numerous clients have, quite literally, plopped down on the couch in front of me and said, "Fix me, and fix me fast!" no matter how many years it took them to reach their current state. I have seen quite a few clients spend an exorbitant amount of energy complaining, whining, and playing the blame game while they continue to swirl in a whirlpool of depression and anxiety. For most, if the same energy was used toward some of the common techniques recommended to eliminate or reduce depression and anxiety, their suffering would be a thing of the past. The quickest and surest way to get out of the pile of shit would be to take action and get yourself out it. The same goes for depression and anxiety.

To be happy is the number one desire for most of my clients. Most believe that happiness is a complicated, convoluted concept that is difficult to acquire. I do not believe this to be true. My experience has taught me that it's really the simple and basic actions that enable one to overcome depression and anxiety and live a happy life. The real issue is that many of us have no idea what happiness means for ourselves. This is what makes obtaining happiness more difficult.

When I ask clients, "What is happiness to you?" I hear two vague, reoccurring phrases: "I just want to be happy," or "I want to be happy like everyone else." With a look of bewilderment, my questions are then: "If you don't know what happiness means to you, how will you know when you have achieved it?" and "Where are you exerting your energy and effort now to acquire happiness?" Are you shooting at random targets and hoping for the best, or do you have a bull's-eye in sight? Are you shooting at anything at all? You are more likely to hit a bull's-eye if you know what you are aiming at it. You are more likely to acquire happiness if you know what makes you happy.

You are more likely to acquire happiness if you have a target, focus in on it, and aim directly at it. The truth is, most of us have never really given much thought to what would make us happy. If you do not know where you are going, any road will get you there. If you aim at nothing, you will hit it every time. This is what leaves many on a fruitless, seemingly never-ending quest for happiness and with the narrow-minded belief that happiness is impossible to attain.

*"**The greatest part of our happiness depends on our dispositions, not our circumstances**."* –Martha Washington

YOU ARE NOT ALONE

When we are going through something for some strange reason we believe that out of the over 7 billion folks in the world, we are the only one experiencing strife, and we feel so alone and isolated. This is so far from the truth. We are all going through something. It is called life.

The number one complaint in my practice is depression, followed by anxiety. The two often go hand in hand. About ***14.8 million*** American adults suffer from some form of depression. Nearly one half of those who suffer with depression also suffer from an anxiety disorder. According to the National Institute of Mental Health, **40 million** US adults suffer from anxiety.

Market Data Enterprises, an independent Tampa-based research firm, reports Americans spent $11 billion in 2008 on self-improvement books, CDs, seminars, coaching, and stress-management programs. Individuals are suffering and looking for help.

CHAPTER TWO – TREATMENT INFORMATION
WHAT IS COGNITIVE BEHAVIORAL THERAPY & SOLUTION-FOCUSED THERAPY?

Over the course of my career, I have heard all kinds of stories, complaints, and problems. When I think I have seen and heard the worst, there always seems to be something that will flip my wig back and make me go "Whoa!" However, I think it is safe to say that much of the unhappiness in our lives stems from distorted perceptions, faulty processing of reality, and poor responses and choices. Some experiences, such as those involving physical and emotional neglect, abuse, rape, grief, and loss, are tragic, horrific, and outside the individual's control. Yet, even in these instances, we have power. We have the power to decide how we perceive, process, and respond to life's events, both good and bad.

I am a huge fan of cognitive behavioral therapy, as most situational depression and anxiety is rooted in distorted thoughts about reality. Cognitive behavioral therapy, or CBT, provides education and awareness into your thoughts and mindset. It focuses on reducing depression and anxiety by challenging and changing core thoughts and beliefs that feed negative emotions, which contribute to a depressed or anxious mood. If you can change your thoughts, your mindset and emotions will change, and subsequently your mood will improve.

Another approach I use quite frequently is solution-focused therapy, or SFT for short. SFT was developed by **Steve de Shaker** and **Insoo Kim Berg** and their colleagues in the late 1970s. It focuses on the present, the future, and what you want in your life. The purpose of reviewing the past is *only* to clarify distortions and identify resources and strengths, especially those used to conquer struggles in the past. Focusing on the solution and not the problem redirects your energy and actions toward problem solving.

Essential to this style and approach is asking yourself miracle questions like, "What would my life look like without the problem I am currently experiencing?" "What would be different?" "What would I be doing that I am not doing right now?" "How would I feel?" "Who would or would not be present?" This provides a good place to start and challenges your mind to focus on what you want, and not what you don't want in your life.

When we are depressed and anxious, we predominately focus on what is wrong and what we don't want, which just leads to more depression and anxiety. SFT is changing "I can't" into "How can I?" When you say "I can't," you're taking the easy way out, which allows you to lay the blame elsewhere and remain stagnant. When you ask, "How can I?" you accept responsibility and start to look for solutions that, in turn, produce results. SFT is often very successful for those who want to move forward and not spend a lot of time reliving the past. I love the way clients' faces light up when they begin to find answers to these questions.

During the first counseling session, I ask four questions. 1) What is it that you are trying to change or would like to improve? 2) Do you want change more than you want to complain? 3) Are you willing to do the work? 4) What are you expecting out of therapy? I ask these four questions to evaluate a client's mindset, because this tells me exactly how to formulate a treatment plan.

Few of us know exactly what needs to change in our lives in order to alleviate depression and anxiety and increase happiness. In the beginning, we are often not really aware of what the exact issue may be. However, just acknowledging that something isn't right is a good place to start and can lead to the discovery of the real issue at hand.

The second question is necessary because some people just want to talk incessantly or whine about what is wrong, and this is all they will ever do. This makes counseling a waste of time, theirs and mine. This frustrates me because there is no better feeling for me than seeing clients overcome their depression and anxiety.

Clients often expect therapists to wave a magic wand and make everything better instantly, even if their problems have been years in the making. It is important to realize that therapy does not work in this way. Being happy takes work, and the onus or responsibility falls on the client, not the therapist. The third question can help clients to realize this.

The fourth question is important because identifying expectations of therapy gives direction and determines whether your desires and goals are achievable. It also helps identify if the therapist has the capacity to help you.

WHAT LEVEL OF THERAPY IS BEST FOR YOU?

There are different levels of treatment available for individuals, couples, and families. Individuals can turn to one-on-one therapy with counselors, therapists, clergy, and life coaches for assistance. With this kind of treatment, you are expected to discuss your problems, learn how to think through your issues critically and rationally, problem-solve, and learn effective coping techniques.

Another type of treatment is medication management. All too often, this is the first and only line of treatment. While I am not a huge advocate of this approach, if your issues impair your ability to function, I recommend medication management. This is best supervised by a psychiatrist, physician assistant, or nurse practitioner (NP). In my professional opinion, it is okay if primary care physicians prescribe simple medications such as a sleep aid. However, I believe that psychiatrists, physician's assistants, and NPs trained in psychiatry should manage medication for mood disorders. If something was wrong with your heart, you would not see a dermatologist. Both are medical doctors, but each specializes in their field. That being said, it is a personal decision as to what type of practitioner you select.

Of note, most psychiatrists, physician's assistants, and NPs do not provide therapy. It is unlikely that you will lie on the leather couch and discuss your early childhood memories with them. Instead, they focus on your symptoms, because their role is to prescribe medication to help manage mental conditions. I have frequently heard from clients, "I did not get a chance to talk about my problems," when they saw a psychiatrist. "I was only in there for 10 minutes and was given a prescription" is another complaint. Psychiatrists, physicians, and NPs are qualified to provide therapy and counseling. However, only a few provide counseling in addition to medication management.

The next level of care is intensive outpatient therapy. In this format, a group meets several days per week for three to four hours a day. This level is for higher functioning individuals who need services that are more intensive. One of the biggest benefits of a group setting is the knowledge that there is someone else experiencing what you are going through and this can make you feel normal. Hearing the struggles of others and seeing them resolve their issues can be cathartic and beneficial for most participants and inspire them to do the same.

A higher level of care is a partial hospitalization program (PHP), which is suggested when individuals are even more acutely affected by their mood disorders. At this level, a lot of structure is necessary for stabilization. Daily group sessions can last anywhere from six to eight hours. It is a step below full inpatient hospitalization.

The criteria for full inpatient hospitalization is having suicidal or homicidal thoughts or ideations and/or psychosis. You may have other serious problems such as anger, maladaptive personality traits, homelessness, drug addiction, and make poor decisions, but these do not meet the criteria for hospitalization in a psychiatric unit. These issues take time to resolve and are best handled by an outpatient provider. The goal of this level of treatment is stabilization and to start patients on the road to recovery. You will not be at 100% with all of your problems solved before you are discharged from the hospital. The key to stabilization and continued recovery is following through with recommendations, which many individuals fail to do.

Ideally, it is good to start with the least restrictive level of care. Most start with therapy on the individual level. If one fails at this level, and it is not due to lack of effort or an ineffective therapist, the next level of care may be necessary.

TEN TIPS TO GET MORE OUT OF THERAPY

Some individuals will spend more time choosing an outfit or a pair of shoes than they do selecting a therapist. This is not the time to say "eeny meeny miny moe" and hope for the best. There are thousands of therapists, but some are better than others. Additionally, there are thousands of theories and treatment styles. It is crucial to find out what works for you. Below are ten tips to improve your chance of having a successful outcome in therapy.

1) Know what type of depression and anxiety you're experiencing.

We are all prone to bouts of sadness, excessive worry, or getting worked up over small things, but we eventually snap out of it. The problem is when we get stuck and camp out with depression and anxiety. There are two types of depression and anxiety. Situational, or endogenous, depression and anxiety are rooted in a situation and caused by an identifiable source or event, such as stress, loss, financial problems, or relationship issues. Exogenous depression and anxiety are biological, or genetic, in nature and can be caused by medications, hormonal changes in the body, foods, and existing ailments such as thyroid conditions. Identifying what type of depression and anxiety you are experiencing determines the most appropriate treatment plan right away.

2) Consider what you want to accomplish in therapy.

Before you reach out to a counselor or therapist, think about what you would like to get out of therapy. As stated previously, therapists are not magicians who can zap all of your troubles away and correct all of your flaws. A good therapist's goal is to help you accurately identify what your issues are, help you think critically and logically, and assist you with developing effective ways to eliminate, manage, or cope with your issue. Having clear goals for treatment helps both you and your therapist monitor progress, indicate if therapy is successful, and lets you know when it is time to end therapy or switch therapists if necessary.

3) Select good sources for referrals.

Ask people you know who are functioning well, or who are in therapy and improving, if they can recommend someone. Friends, medical providers, and those in the mental health field are additional resources. Be selective with who you ask for assistance; not everyone has your best interests at heart. There are those who want to find out your business so they can have something to talk about, those who will start talking about their own issues, and those who cannot think outside the box for themselves, let alone for you. This is not what you need when you are depressed and anxious.

4) Keep in mind that therapy is a unique experience.

What worked for your friend may not necessarily work for your situation. Your treatment plan should be personalized with goals and objectives constructed especially for the unique individual that you are.

5) Interview the therapist.

If possible, the initial phone call to your chosen therapist's office should be more like a brief interview rather than a call to automatically schedule an appointment. Do not expect to take up more than five to ten minutes of the therapist's time. Most practitioners have very tight schedules and you should not try to get a free counseling session. The goal is to get a feel as to whether the therapist you're considering understands your issue(s) and whether you two connect or relate to each other. This is called a therapeutic bond. If there is no bond with your therapist, it does not mean that therapy itself does not work; it simply means that this particular therapist is not a good fit for you.

My ideology and focus in therapy is self-empowerment. It is my goal to help clients learn that they already have the tools to help themselves. The tools may need a little sharpening, but most of us have the capacity to learn how to manage our issues and become independent, not dependent on a therapist. When clients thank me at the end of therapy or when we do a progress check, I remind them to pat themselves on the back because they did the work. I just guided them.

Make sure there is a bond with your therapist. If not, look for a new therapist. I do not click with every client I encounter, and I explain this in our introduction. A while ago, I realized I relate to, and I am most effective with, common, everyday people. This is who I am and most of my knowledge and effectiveness with clients come from life, not just my education and training.

Several years ago I met with a Harvard-educated, privileged gentleman presenting with anxiety. We both agreed that there was nothing wrong, we just did not connect with each other, and it was not a good fit. I referred him to someone else. I did the same thing for another gentleman who wanted me to be available to him practically every day to work through every little issue he encountered throughout the course of his day.

I have a life and must compartmentalize my days. If I'm in therapist mode at every moment, I will burn out and need therapy myself. I also referred him to another practitioner. It is important that a therapist knows what is beyond their scope of practice. When a client who presented for depression revealed that he had a sexual addiction and that he performed oral sex on his mother while his father watched, I referred him to someone who specializes in sexual issues. This was way beyond my scope of practice.

If you read the bios of therapists, sometimes you will find a lengthy list of conditions they treat. I did this in my early days, but then I decided to focus on what I was really good at, and that boiled down to about five conditions. Find a therapist who has experience with your issues. Would you want to be a surgeon's first patient? No, you want someone with experience.

Further, if you find that a therapist is clueless about your culture and your unique experiences, and their only source of knowledge about you comes from a textbook, it might be wise to say, "Thank you for your time," and move on quickly. I cannot stress enough the importance of making sure a therapist has experience with your issues, can separate their personal values from yours, and can be objective. It is okay to get another therapist if it is not working out for you. The therapist should not get mad if you leave and go somewhere else, and if they do, you are making the right move.

6) Know what therapy entails.

A good therapist is a neutral, confidential party who helps you explore your strengths and weaknesses, logically examine areas of concern, check out how you have been handling the matter, and develop ways to resolve issues. However, once you have the tools, awareness, and resources to begin improving your life, it is your responsibility to apply them.

Too many people arrive at therapy with a "fix me" attitude and have no intention of doing any real work. The therapist should not work harder than you to fix your life, so be sure you are willing to put in the time, commitment, and effort necessary.

7) Be willing to take a look at yourself.

As I've said before, individuals often don't know what is really bothering them. They might think it is a superficial issue, and it is usually something much deeper. For example, a wife's complaint of her husband's inattentiveness and uncaring nature may really be about her own unmet needs from childhood that she's trying to resolve through her husband, who may not have the capacity to fulfill those needs. Discussing your goals will help you and your therapist develop a realistic and achievable plan for your future, and this may include looking at your situation from a different perspective and taking actions you might not have considered before.

8) Understand that the locus of change is within you.

Countless clients have come into my office to rant about how someone in their life needs to change, repeatedly asking why the other person can't just see things their way. I say, "Who are you to tell anyone what he or she needs to do?" Isn't it more than enough effort to try to keep your own wig on straight and run your own life, much less expend energy running around, trying to tell others what to do? Understand, everyone has free will, and just because someone disagrees with you does not automatically make him or her wrong or a bad person. If you have all the answers, why isn't your life perfect? The only person you can change is you, and the sooner you accept this, the faster you'll progress. Your own life is more than enough to handle. Stay in your lane and focus on you.

9) Complete the tasks and assignments given to you.

Clients are usually given a task or a homework assignment to complete between sessions. These are an important part of your treatment plan, as they often lead to improvement outside therapy. Not completing these tasks may delay your progress and potentially exacerbate whatever issue(s) you're trying to overcome. You won't get much out of therapy if you don't take every aspect seriously. In my practice, if a client repeatedly insists that they did not have time to complete assignments, yet eagerly reports the same complaint repeatedly, I eventually drop them.

10) Want, and work toward, success.

The most important factor to succeeding in therapy is a desire to get better. You have to want a better life and want it with everything you have. If you give up at the slightest hurdle, or put forth only minimal effort, I say you really do not want it bad enough. If you are committed and serious, nothing will stop you from obtaining and maintaining a life free from depression and anxiety. Take responsibility and direct your life toward success instead of just hoping and wishing for it. Push past the fears and anxiety that come with change, and give as much time to a new way of thinking as you gave to your destructive ways. If you keep doing what you've always done, you'll keep getting what you you've always gotten. You cannot plant weeds and expect roses to pop up.

"It's your road, and yours alone. Others can walk it with you, but no one can walk it for you." –Rumi

CHAPTER THREE – DEPRESSION & ANXIETY 101
HOW DEPRESSION AND ANXIETY FEED OFF OF EACH OTHER

Depression and anxiety are psychologically and biologically interrelated. They feed off of each other. The scenario usually goes like this: You become depressed or stressed over an event, situation or person. You focus most, if not all, of your attention on the negative aspects of this event, situation, or person. You start to generalize the negative thoughts, generalizing or transporting them to other areas of your life. After all this focus on the negative, you start to become anxious and worried. Now you are restless and keyed up. This often leaves you staring at the ceiling when your head hits your pillow, because your mind is racing and you can't turn it off. The next day, fatigue and worry plague you, and eventually you feel helpless, sad, and depressed.

Physiologically, depression and anxiety continue even after the stressful event has ended. Toxins released in response to depression and anxiety can damage your digestive system. These toxins enter your bloodstream and keep you in this state, resulting in a negative feedback loop. Chronic or long-term depression, anxiety, and stress affect every organ system in your body, especially the digestive and immune systems.

DEPRESSION FYI

With depression, you really don't care about anything. As I stated earlier, there are two types of depression: endogenous (situational) and exogenous (biological). Situational depression is endogenous and rooted in a situation caused by an identifiable source such as stress, loss, health-related issues, finances, loneliness, or relationship problems. It involves focusing on the negative aspects of a situation, event, or person or worrying about what might happen and overthinking things.

Exogenous depression is biological or genetic in nature. Examples are depression caused by hormonal changes, medication, PMS, birth control pills, diet, pregnancy, childbirth, menopause, or genetics. Individuals with exogenous depression usually have a family history of depression and anxiety. If a close relative experienced exogenous depression, you have a 15% higher chance of developing depression than individuals without a family history of the illness.

Depression is the leading cause of disability for individuals aged 15 to 44 in the US and is more prevalent in women than men. Clinically, when we speak of depression, we're not talking about a bad day. We are talking about a loss of interest or pleasure in activities you used to enjoy, feelings of guilt, hopelessness, and worthlessness, and suicidal thoughts over an extended period of time that impair your ability to function daily. It is very important to know what type of depression you are dealing with so that a treatment plan can be tailored to you. Best outcomes for depression result from a combination of therapy and sometimes medication.

Below is a chart showing the ways women and men tend to express depression differently.

Women tend to	**Men tend to**
Blame themselves	Feel angry, irritable, and ego inflated
Feel sad, apathetic, and worthless	Retreat to themselves
Feel anxious and scared	Feel suspicious and guarded
Avoid conflicts at all costs	Create conflicts
Feel slowed down and nervous	Feel restless and agitated
Have trouble setting boundaries	Need to feel in control at all costs
Find it easy to talk about self-doubt	Find it "weak" to admit self-doubt or despair
Use food, friends, and "love" to self-medicate	Use alcohol, TV, sports, and sex to self-medicate

Adapted from Male Menopause by Jed Diamond

ANXIETY FYI

With anxiety, you care too much. Anxiety is also both endogenous (situational) and exogenous (biological). There are several forms of anxiety. Generalized anxiety, panic attacks, posttraumatic stress disorder, social anxiety, and phobias are the most common. Women are twice as likely as men to be affected. Clinical symptoms include feeling overwhelmed, excessive worry, difficulty controlling worry, and at least three of the following: restlessness, fatigue, irritability, muscle tension, difficulty sleeping or concentrating which impairs daily living, and interference with work, school, or social functioning.

There are a variety of causes of anxiety. Some people are just naturally anxious, but anxiety can also be caused by environmental factors such as a traumatic event, history of abuse, victimization, death of a loved one, difficult relationships, and other stressors.

Much of anxiety centers on worrying about the unknown, being cynical or pessimistic, and believing the worst is going to happen without respect to facts or proof. It has been said that 80% of what we worry about does not happen and the 20% that does is usually not as bad as we thought it would be. Genetically or through learned behavior, humans seem to have a need to know what's ahead. One can only try to predict the future. No one can absolutely guarantee what will happen tomorrow, and this causes a lot of anxiety.

Personally, I believe the increase in anxiety comes from our fast-paced society, and we are simply doing too much. We are worried, keyed up, and restless because our minds are racing about what we have to do.

We live in a time when technology is supposed to make our lives easier, but is life really getting any simpler? We are constantly in "on mode," and we do not know how to turn it off. For example, do you ever turn your cell phone off? Most of us do not. This makes you "on" all the time. Have you ever answered a call and had to explain that you were on vacation? Back in the day, there was no cell phone to take with you. You got the messages when you returned home. Now it is expected that if someone calls you, you will answer the call wherever you are. If you don't, people will "blow up your phone." When you see them, you hear, "Why didn't you answer your phone?" This scenario usually creates anxiety for both parties.

I turn my phone off most evenings and weekends. Do people gripe? Absolutely! However, I need my downtime. I need to reset my nervous system instead of being on adrenal mode or "do and do" mode all time.

It is crucial to understand the type of anxiety you are experiencing, because the type dictates the proper treatment for an optimal outcome. Anxiety is very treatable with therapy by working on solutions to improve whatever is contributing to these conditions. However, sometimes meds are in order.

CHAPTER FOUR – WHAT I HAVE SEEN
MY OBSERVATIONS OF SITUATIONAL DEPRESSION AND ANXIETY

Throughout my career, I've noticed several patterns in my encounters with clients who are battling depression and anxiety. I have found these patterns to be common in both sexes and across cultures.

Many clients experiencing situational depression and anxiety are quick to help others, and are often very good at it, but feel guilty and struggle when it is time to help themselves. Though it is admirable to put your partner, children, family, friends, and your job before yourself, it is not a wise choice when it becomes a detriment to your own quality of life. It is especially bad if it leaves you feeling like crap.

Another pattern I have noticed is that individuals experiencing depression and anxiety sometimes have lives filled with a lot of mess. Clients will describe a laundry list of problems in their lives yet appear clueless as to why they feel like crap. This is how I developed the title of this book. The "mess" is feeling and looking tired, constantly feeling stressed and overwhelmed. Mess can also include moods of sadness, internal and external anger, and depression. Behaviors include incongruence with self or not being the real or authentic you, feelings of ill will towards others, involvement in toxic relationships, vindictiveness, being controlling and manipulative, and malicious behavior.

We cope with the mess by distorting reality, with negative or pessimistic thinking, by holding on to the remnants of past abuse, by allowing others to treat us like we are their toilet bowls, and by using alcohol or drugs. All of this is can be expressed in toxic and unfulfilling relationships, engaging in unproductive stress, having poor self-esteem and low self-worth, a lack of goals or anything to look forward to, or not knowing what your purpose in life is. All this mess feeds depression and anxiety.

Depressed and anxious individuals seem to hold onto mess that is counterproductive to their well-being like it is a 24-karat gold nugget. In spite of a plethora of available help in the form of self-help books, motivational speakers, therapists, inspirational posts on social media, and other tools that help us live happy lives, we cling to useless, unproductive behaviors. We come up with one excuse after another and act like invalids, incapable of helping ourselves. No matter how many lifelines are thrown their way, some continue to spend an exorbitant amount of energy bemoaning how hard it is to overcome depression and anxiety, complaining relentlessly about everything that is wrong and unfair, and pointing fingers at everyone but themselves. Focusing on what is wrong simply leads to more depression.

One last observation I have also noticed is that often depressed and anxious individuals live a life filled with activities they have to do. There are few activities that bring them pleasure or are just plain old fun. There is nothing new or adventurous and this can be boring, mundane, and depressing.

My sister is the poster child for adventure. Around age 40 she decided to take on things she sucked at. My sister could not run, so she joined a run group and now runs marathons. Kim seemed to be having so much fun running, I decided to give it a try and got hooked. She could not swim and decided to take swimming lessons. Her marriage vows consisted of promising to produce one meal a week that did not come out of the microwave because she could not cook, so she enrolled in culinary school.

When my oldest daughter was born, my sister had just returned home from traveling the slave route backwards. She made it to Northern Africa. While holding my newborn daughter, she sighed, "I'm bored, I want to go to Peru." A couple of weeks later, my sister was in Peru. Last year, she camped out with seals in Antarctica, lived in Argentina for seven months, and took my daughter to Panama for three weeks. Spring break she is headed to Paris and for the entire summer she will be in Japan. What I love about my sister is she does not sit around and talk about doing things, nor does she wait for someone to do it with her. She just does it. No, she is not rich. She is an English professor who just lives out her dreams. The point is she takes responsibility for her life, makes life new and adventurous, and does what makes her happy. Anyone who knows her can clearly tell what makes her happy.

What does a typical day or week look like for you? It's filled with routine things, things you have to do, getting the children ready, dropping them off, work and/or school, picking up the children, homework, dinner, cleaning, bills, and sleep, leaving little time for yourself or time for fun, relaxing, and enjoyable activities. Is your life filled with draining and unsupportive relationships, family drama, old scripts, nagging, negative thoughts that play over in our heads, low self-esteem, low self-worth, working too much, not working enough, or a dead-end job? Mix in insecurity, fears, unmet needs from childhood, and baggage from old relationships. So many of us are clogged up with so much mess, it should be no surprise that we are dragging and depressed and anxious. If nothing in your life reflects peace, tranquility, serenity, joy, or love – all the elements of happiness – how in the world can you be happy?

CHAPTER FIVE – LET'S GET STARTED
HEALING THROUGH EXAMPLE

The following are fictional accounts based on real clients I have worked with over the years. Amongst these stories are a few tidbits about myself and how I deal with my own personal issues. Ultimately, it is my goal for you to come across a story you identify with and to see that we are all struggling with something and trying to make it through this thing called life. It's not just you. I want you, the reader, to see how others find the wherewithal to overcome their depression and anxiety and use the stories as a resource to help find solutions to your own issues.

As you read, ask yourself the Solution-Focused Miracle Questions. If I didn't focus on my problems, how would my life be different? How would my life be different if I were not depressed and anxious? What would I be doing that I am not doing now? How would I feel? Who would be present in my life and who needs to go? The answers to these questions will point you in the right direction to turn your life around.

Before asking yourself the miracle questions, it is good to take a look at what is right in your life. This should reveal that your entire life is not all doom and gloom. It also reveals that most of us have what Dr. Fred Luskin of Stanford University calls "champagne problems" – problems that are really not that bad in the grand scheme of things. We tend to magnify our problems and make them out to be much worse than they really are.

Dr. Luskin of Stanford University studies happiness and forgiveness, which I think is the coolest job in the world. He worked with Catholic and Protestant mothers who lost their children in the civil war. They were asked to rate their hurt and pain, and the average rating was 8.8 out of 10. The project then asked members of the general community in the US to rate their hurt and pain, which usually related to something like a boyfriend lying to them or not having the best parents. The average score was 8.6, very close to the hurt and pain rating of burying a loved one in the bloody civil war. Surely a boyfriend lying to you does not compare to burying a child. Yet in our minds, we think our hurt and pain is high because it is happening to us.

We have a lot to be thankful for, but we fail to appreciate what we have. According to Luskin, being grateful, along with forgiving, increases happiness. You could live in a third-world country without shelter or enough food or clean water but you don't. Someone who had trouble finding work would love to have the job you complain about. If there were rumors of lay-offs pending, how would you feel about your job? There are others who are more fortunate than you, yet there are others who would kill to have what you possess. It is far more uplifting to be grateful and appreciative.

How do you expand what is right and what is already working well in your life? If you say there is nothing right in your life, which is a thought depressed and anxious individuals often have, could you simply be grateful for the fact that you are alive? Consider that you have talents and skills that enabled you to survive up to this point. Think about someone with a terminal illness who would give anything to live. Someone without legs is yearning to have them.

If you feel you would be better off if you were not alive, please consider this: most clients with suicidal thoughts simply want relief, some want attention. Do not make a permanent decision for a temporary problem. If you have suicidal thoughts, call 911 immediately or go to the nearest hospital. Call a friend. Trust and believe that this too shall pass. If a situation is causing you depression and anxiety, in the end, this period will be a mere blip in the grand scheme of your entire life.

This book deals with many issues — sexual assault, self-esteem, health issues, family problems, addiction, anxiety and stress, and relationships. You will observe that most end happily, a few not so happily, and some have no ending at all. This is life, not TV.

"Life has many chapters. One bad chapter does not mean it is the end of the book." –Kashif Shani

ANXIETY

As stated earlier, anxiety disorders can develop from a plethora of things: genetics, brain chemistry, personality, and life events. Some people are naturally anxious because they were predisposed to be. Others learn anxious behavior from caregivers, and for most, the root of their anxiety is the reliving of an unchangeable past or fear of an unknowable future. The hectic pace of western society, where multitasking is an admired prerequisite in many of our roles at home, work, and school, is also a contributing factor.

Or you can be like some of my clients who spend their time doing nothing all day? This contributes to a great deal of loneliness and sadness because all they'll do is sit around and think about what is wrong with their lives, and feed and fatten depression and anxiety.

The reality is that surviving each day is becoming more difficult for most of us. Frequent violence in the news, increased demands at work, and constant fears of job loss is counterintuitive to our biological need for stability. Many of us live paycheck-to-paycheck and are one paycheck away from ending up in the streets. Too often we set ourselves up for failure by knowingly taking on too much and beating ourselves up for not accomplishing everything. Have you ever told yourself you can get something done in 30 minutes, but in reality you know you need an hour? Then you beat yourself up because you did not get it done? I use to do this all the time.

We are on the go all the time and set aside little or no time to relax, refresh, or reset from our hectic lifestyles. Furthermore, safety nets that cushioned stress continue to vanish as the cohesiveness of families and communities breaks down and the availability of social services and informal support decline. For example, neighbors were once a common source of support. Now, most of us are not intimately acquainted with our neighbors as we were in the past. I worked with a gentleman from Iraq, who suffered from cultural isolation. He shared that everything here is rush, rush, rush, and he was having problems adjusting to the pace. My reply, "Honestly sir, the pace is not working too well for us either." No doubt, the factors listed above and more, are taking a toll on our minds and bodies.

As humans, we want to know. We want to know what is around the corner, what's ahead, what's going on, what the future holds. Much of anxiety stems from a fear of the unknown. This is why the dark is so frightening. Again, most of what we worry about does not occur, and what does occur is frequently not as bad as we thought it would be. While it is good to plan and be prepared – and that includes preparing for the worst-case scenario we are worried about – it is not good when we dwell or ruminate on something to the point that it causes us to be depressed and anxious. It is far better and more effective to plan for the future than to not worry about it.

It is time to stop feeding depression and anxiety. The most beneficial thing you can do for anxiety and depression is to take care of yourself and make yourself a priority. One thing that people often neglect is SELF – sleep, exercise, leisure, and food.

It might be difficult, but a good night's sleep can leave you refreshed, as opposed to being fatigued and on edge. In order to sleep, you need to be relaxed. No one can go to sleep while tense and hyped up. Know your sleep pressure (the need to sleep) and sleep cycle. If you don't have one, work on developing a sleep routine. Wind down several hours before bedtime instead of working up until it's time to hit the sack or you can't do another thing.

Starting a moderate exercise routine for at least three days a week will not only help you get in shape, but can also calm the mind and release endorphins that help you feel better. A moderate exercise regimen where the heart rate is increased for at least 30 minutes will affect the same hormones that anti-depressant and anti-anxiety medications affect and without side effects.

Engage in activities that you enjoy, because a life of doing only what we have to do becomes mundane and depressing. Take a class or pursue a hobby. The goal is to keep the mind active and have something to look forward to each day.

Eat a well-balanced meal so the body has the fuel to handle the day's demands. You have heard it a thousand times: eat more fruits and vegetables. Drink plenty of water.

Self-care is the foundation to feeling better. Don't have time to do these things? I suggest you find time. If not, stop complaining about your condition if you are not going to do anything about it.

Other helpful techniques: Be careful of your thoughts at the start of the day. Your mindset at the top of the day, particularly the first 30 minutes of the day, will set the tone for the rest of your day. Start the day off by exercising if you can. Meditation, mantras, and prayer can also be very beneficial. Saying no and setting boundaries is difficult for most people because individuals often find it hard to handle the repercussions of saying no, whether it is someone becoming mad at them or the guilt that can arise. Examine and plan how to deal with what comes up when you say no.

Recently I have defected from the "be strong" camp, because I am seeing the side effects of being strong. More and more individuals seeking therapy are overwhelmed, stressed, unhappy, stuck in a rut, and even become suicidal trying to be strong. Equally alarming is the noticeable increase I have seen in the number of first-time psychiatric admissions for major depression and suicidal ideations or attempts. Many of these individuals ignored the physical and emotional alarms set off by the body to make adjustments in their lives, kept pushing, and then were blindsided by the breaking point.

I'm not saying that you should neglect responsibilities. We all have to eat, have shelter, and provide for our families, but we have to love and nurture ourselves routinely and consistently as we handle everything else. Take a step back, and do not allow yourself to become consumed. I had a client who was the primary caregiver for his mother who had dementia. He said, "I take a vacation every day." He takes a break and resets every day. I find it relaxing to debrief from the craziness at work each day. Sometimes I will go by the park or lake before going home. It is my way of turning off work mode and preparing for wife and mommy mode when I get home. Eventually, you will discover that you can never complete everything on the "to do" list, you can never make enough money, for the most part, and some pursuits are just not worth it.

EDWARD

I know I suffer from anxiety. The anxiety makes me depressed and I cry a lot. My brother calls me a big crybaby, and my mother just does not understand. I just get so tearful and hopeless. I want to get better.
I know I cry a lot, and I don't know why. I just do. Sometimes I get frightened and I have panic attacks. The panic attacks are the worst. They hold me back and stop me from doing anything. All I want to do is lock myself up in the house and not deal with life and pretend the world outside isn't there.

There is nothing I can do about my anxiety, no matter how hard I try. Every time I start working on my problems, I get scared, and my anxiety takes over, and I begin to doubt myself. I've been to therapy before. I've heard about all the exercises and routines that you can do to help yourself. I just don't think about them when I'm depressed and anxious. The only thing that makes me feel better is watching TV, listening to my music, and playing video games, because they block the world out and take me away from reality.

I know what I'm doing isn't fair to my wife, and she is getting fed up and frustrated with me. She is tired of carrying the load for our family and wants me to get a job and help the household financially. My wife still stands by me; I don't know why, but she does. I really don't deserve her. I want to work and I want to go to school but my anxiety prevents me from doing this.

When I feel anxious, it feels like I'm dying, so I call my wife at work, panicking, not knowing what to do. She rushes home, concerned, and gets mad when there is nothing really wrong with me. It makes me feel better when she comes to see about me. I don't know what else to do when my anxiety strikes. Playing my video games and listening to music really helps me self-soothe.

The Mess

Edward held onto, and lived out, every aspect of his anxiety diagnosis. In my notes, I referred to him as Mr. Anxiety. In my opinion, being anxious and depressed came with some pretty good benefits. He commented he liked being a stay-at-home dad, but his mother kept his son more than he did.

Edward's Mindset

In Edward's mind, being anxious justified his refusal to work or fulfill any responsibilities, like working, contributing to the household, helping his wife, and taking care of their son. He is solely focused on finding the right medication to conquer his anxiety, even though he has been on several meds.

Miracle Question Response

I would not be anxious.

Solution

Starting with what is going right in his life, in his late thirties, Edward has a supportive wife of 5 years, a roof over his head, a wife holding down the fort, and supportive family members, despite his behavior. Edward learned several techniques to manage his anxiety, such as opposite action. Opposite action is one of the most effective techniques to get you moving and get you into action when you are not motivated. If you don't feel like getting out of bed, you do so anyway. The opposite of just lying in bed is getting out of bed. You do so because it is in your best interest to get out of bed. Getting into action can precede motivation. You will miss out on life and remain stuck in depression and anxiety if you keep waiting for the right moment to do something.

Distraction is another technique taught to Edward. Distraction is engaging in a positive activity that requires your attention instead of ruminating or occupying your mind with something negative over and over again. Examples of distraction are watching TV, reading a book, doing a crossword puzzle, or engaging in any positive activity. In sum, just occupy your mind with something besides what you are worried about.

Edward's depression and anxiety did not lessen or resolve itself, and I don't believe it ever will if he maintains his current mindset and behavior. Honestly, I believe secondary gains were at play. Secondary gains are the benefits of being depressed and anxious. Yes, there can be benefits from being depressed and anxious. Being depressed and anxious can get you out of activities and responsibilities, and it can get you attention.

According to Edward, he could not work because of his depression and anxiety. He could not take care of their son because of his depression and anxiety. He could not do any household chores because of depression and anxiety. He could not make friends because of it. He could not apply any of the techniques presented in therapy because of his depression and anxiety. Had Edward at least attempted to apply some of the techniques, I would have a different opinion of him. Additionally, his mother and two of his siblings also suffered from anxiety but manage to perform activities of daily living and hold down employment. Three of his siblings did not suffer from anxiety. It can be questioned whether the anxiety is hereditary or a learned behavior.

STEVE

I'm so anxious, it keeps me awake at night, and I can't stop worrying about work. My job is so stressful. It's one project deadline after another. These 70- and 80-hour work weeks are killing me. I haven't had a good night's sleep for quite some time. Right now, I am just not coping well. I don't know why, all of a sudden, my lifestyle is a problem. I'm happily married. I have a wonderful job and two great kids. I should be a happy guy.

I'm not the only one complaining about the pace of work. Other guys on my team are complaining too. One guy quit. No one wants to be the first one to speak up and say something to management. I can't handle it! I'm just so tired from the lack of sleep. All night I toss and turn. Before you know it, it's time to get up. Really, I'm not sure if I'm depressed – never really been depressed before.

Okay, maybe I do have a problem. Maybe I do need medication. I'll see a psychiatrist. I just don't want to become dependent on anything. Medication does not make problems go away. I'm just so tired and groggy. I need sleep so badly, but as soon as my head hits the pillow, all I do is worry over and over about the job and my wife. Usually I'll fall asleep around four in the morning, and I'm only getting about 3 hours of sleep a night. I wake up. The problems are still there; they haven't gone away. My concentration is off all day, and it is difficult to focus on anything for any length of time. Throughout the entire day I just drag along. I try to put on a happy face but inside I feel like I'm dying.

I wish I could fix my sick wife. It's what I do. I solve problems. But this one is out of my control, and I feel so powerless. I made a promise to take care of her. I made a promise to be there for her, but I have failed her. I have let her down, and I can't handle that. I can't watch her go through her cancer treatments knowing that there's nothing I can do to make her better. I know I would never forgive myself if something happened to her, if she took a turn for the worse and I wasn't there for her, but I just don't have the strength.

At work, I am in control. I am highly regarded and respected, and the company has been good to me. So I just keep at it, making sure I'm putting in the hours, making sure I'm doing my duty as a provider. I know the workload is tough. I know the hours are unrealistic, but I cannot give up. I am no quitter. Many guys in my unit want to quit. I have a few contacts and other companies, but this is such a great company to work for, and I really don't want to leave.

I hate that I'm not around much for my boys. I love them. I really enjoy when we spend time together. There are just not enough hours in the day. I've got to put the hours in to stay on top at work.

The Mess

Steve suffered from anxiety, depression, guilt, role overload, a fear of failure, and constant worry. He was a perfectionist.

Steve's Mindset

He had to be perfect and in control of every aspect of his life, otherwise he felt like a failure. He took everything seriously and was always on guard, trying to maintain his competent, dependable, good-guy image. He never wanted be perceived as incompetent or not on top of things. Every "i" had to be dotted, and every "t" had to be crossed, and he would always be the one to do it.

Miracle Question Response

I would have more time for myself and with my family, especially my wife. I enjoy my job, and I am loyal to my employer, where I have been employed for fifteen years, but the 70- to 80-hour work weeks are taking their toll on me. Working fewer hours would be great.

Solution

Steve has a beautiful family, a good career, and is a good provider, husband, and father. He is also a caring and spiritual person. I suggested that Steve consider exploring opportunities at other companies, but he never did. He was not amenable to considering less stressful positions with his existing employer or going to management to ask for a lighter load so he could deal with his wife's illness. To compromise, we decided it was acceptable to work late, but he needed to be totally devoted to his family on the weekend. This meant no work on the weekend, no checking work e-mails, and no pursuing ideas that popped into his head. If he got a bright idea, he was to write it down and table it until the next work day.

Because his anxiety impaired his daily functioning, I referred Steve to a psychiatrist who prescribed anti-anxiety medications and a sleep aid. He also agreed to start practicing mindfulness as a way to address worries about the future. Mindfulness is a simple technique which involves staying in the present moment and not worrying about the future or living in a past you cannot change. Focusing on the present moment and acknowledging that you are safe and okay can help calm the mind and bring you back to center instead of getting you more worked up.

As recommended, Steve started listening to something positive en route to work in the mornings. He chose one of my favorites, Charles Stanley of In Touch Ministries. A positive and encouraging word at the beginning of the day helped set the tone for his day.

Maybe it was the introduction to medication, therapy, or both, but a light bulb went off for Steve. One day, Steve walked into the session looking like he had discovered gold. He was brighter, no longer tearful or looking down at the floor when he talked. He decided that if something went wrong with a project at work, instead of feeling guilty or like a failure, he would accept that he could simply turn to his team and have faith that, together, they would find a solution. Steve started planning weekend activities with his family and spending time with his wife and his boys. Subsequently, he terminated therapy. About eight weekly sessions was all he needed to get his life back on track, and he no longer needed therapy.

"Over-thinking ruins you. Ruins the situation, twists things around, makes you worry and just makes everything much worse than it actually is." – Author unknown

MONICA

Am I having a nervous breakdown? I am so tired, anxious, and so depressed all the time. And the panic attacks leave me exhausted, mentally and physically. Right now I'm having 3 to 4 attacks a day. I know I am scattered and all over the place. It's so overwhelming that I feel stuck and paralyzed. I can't go on like this. There is just so much to do. I'm always running here, running there. There are not enough hours in the day. Working 70- and 80-hour weeks is killing me. As an accountant, I have to be exact, right on the money with everything. Everything has to be exact. I want to prove to management that I can handle my job, and I am the one they can count on to handle any situation.

I'm trying so hard to keep it together, to provide for and support my daughter, and keep her in private school. We really don't have quality time together because I'm always at work so much. I do the best I can with what I have. This is a one-woman show. It is up to me to make it happen. If I don't, who will?

Really, I'm not coping well. I'm making too many mistakes at work. Now I'm being watched like a hawk watches its prey. I noticed I'm getting less and less work assigned to me. A colleague told me the manager is trying to make me quit. I feel so scattered. I don't know what to do. Right now, I just can't stop crying, and there is no way I can return to that job. I am empty, and I just can't go back to the job.

I hate my job anyway, but the money is good, and it pays the bills. To be honest, I really want to go back to school and be a nurse or a teacher or something. I'm not sure. Maybe I could get a less stressful job and go to school part-time. I just need to keep pushing. I just need to find myself. I don't want anyone to see that I can't handle things.

When I have my attacks, I have to run to the bathroom. I have it all, shortness of breath, heart palpitations, tremors, and sweats. It really feels like a heart attack. They are starting to happen more frequently. Right now, I'm having between five and seven panic attacks a day, and it's so exhausting.

I must admit that I have days when I feel I am returning to that dark place. I want to cut so bad just to get some relief. I used to be a really bad cutter. Maybe I should just take some pills, go to sleep, and end the misery, but my daughter needs me. I know I have to get help! I really don't want to end my life. I just want some relief. My daughter needs me. I just don't know what to do.

The Mess

Monica is exhausted, emotionally and physically, due to lack of self-care. She has pushed and pushed, even though her mind and body have told her she is exhausted and something has to give. In her late thirties, I believe there is some incongruence with her real self. She is not pursuing what is true to her heart and living the life she really wants.

Monica's Mindset

Monica has to prove she is capable. If she doesn't do it, who will? Follow her dreams and passion? "Oh, I'll do that later."

Miracle Question Response

I want to be at home more with my boyfriend and my beautiful daughter. (When she spoke of them, a warm smile crept on to her face). There would be more family time and family activities. We would eat dinner together, and we would go places. Also, I would not get flustered so easily at work. I think I want to be a nurse. I like helping people. I know I have to work, so returning to school on a part-time basis would be good. I don't know what I want to do. I want to have the strength to push myself.

Solution

Monica has good support and a loving and caring family. This is worth more than gold. Most of all, she has skills and opportunities. She has been in her field for ten years. I was on board with her desires until she said she needed to push herself. This is what led to a psychological breakdown. It would be better for her to take some time off from work to get herself together. The frantic pace had taken its toll on her, and now it was time to rest and reset. I advised Monica to postpone any major decisions, like quitting her job. You could see her shoulders drop when I told her some time off was in order.

Incorporating a SELF-routine was crucial for Monica. Again, SELF stands for sleep, exercise, leisure, and food. She was to work on improving each one of these on a daily basis until they became habitual. To further move toward healing, it was also beneficial for her to do what brought a smile to her face, and that included spending more time with family. The goal was not to be stronger but to work smarter. If she decides to return to her job, it was suggested she work some overtime but put a limit to the number of hour she would work. It was the middle of the school semester, and she could not start school immediately, but Monica could start looking into what she needed to do to become a nurse. She could also engage in career exploration to see what careers might be a good fit for her. Working in accounting paid the bills, which is necessary, but her heart had been in nursing for a long time. She could view her present job as a stepping stone to doing what she really wanted. It would cost nothing to shadow a nurse to see if this was something she truly wanted to pursue.

Often, when something is wrong, one of the first things we blame is our job. Yes, jobs can suck, but often it's not the job, it is us. If you make the necessary changes in your life and take care of yourself and the job still sucks, it may be the job. Learn to appreciate your job. Imagine not having that job for a year. Think about the struggles you would have not being employed for a year. How would you feel about your job? I am appreciative of my job. At times it does suck, but it allows me to keep a roof over my head and provide for my children, and I am grateful for this.

Monica also needed to learn to set boundaries and say no. Anything that interfered with her happiness, family time, returning to school, or anything else where the cost outweighed the benefits or caused her extreme distress had to go. It was either on the way or in the way, and if it was in the way, it had to go. Monica is doing well. She enrolled in an intensive outpatient program for mood disorders and is learning coping skills.

"Make yourself a priority once in a while. It is not selfish. It is necessary." –Author unknown

STRESSED AND OVERWHELMED

Technically, there isn't a clinical diagnosis for stress in the American Psychological Association's Diagnostic and Statistical Manual of Mental Disorders (DSM). The DSM classifies acute stress disorder, which relates to exposure to a traumatic event but not the stress that comes from being overwhelmed. The DSM definition is not what most of us have in mind when we think of stress.

I remember informing my primary care physician that I was under a great deal of stress, working four, sometimes five, jobs to provide for my children and to make sure my daughter remained in an exclusive private girls' school. He gave me a diagnosis of anxiety and a prescription for Xanax. I threw the prescription in the trash can outside of the medical office building and fussed all the way to my car that I was not anxious, I was stressed. It took a lot for me to realize and accept that I was stressed out. I thought: If he was going to give me a diagnosis, give me one that I could collect a check for.

There should be a clinical diagnosis for stress, but stress is classified under anxiety. I returned to my hectic pace for a couple more years until my multiple projects and side hustles dropped off one by one until there were only two. I did not have sense enough to quit, so I believe God eliminated what was necessary to prevent me from digging my own grave. I knew this pace was killing me slowly, but the "need more" mentality kept me saying yes to any opportunity that came my way. The body will adapt to whatever pace you set, healthy and unhealthy. I have learned to say no quite well, and my world did not end, nor did we wind up in the poorhouse. We have fared just fine. Now I look back and do not know how I managed that pace for as long as I did.

Job and relationship stress is what individuals present to therapy most often. Stress – real or imagined – is a normal physical response when you feel threatened. It is one of the body's alarm systems to prompt you to make adjustments. The stress response is necessary for survival and for a fight-or-flight reaction. Either do something or run. Major life changes (even positive ones), financial problems, family responsibilities, relationships, school, and work can cause stress. The stress, in turn, causes excessively worry, pessimism, and starts a pattern of negative thought cycling, unrealistic expectations, perfectionism, and black-and-white thinking.

There is good stress and bad stress. Good stress helps you rise to the occasion. It helps you to be sharp, increases your concentration, aides in problem-solving, and gets you through difficult situations. I do some of my best thinking when my back is against the wall.

Stress can also be harmful, particularly if it is chronic and long-term. Long-term stress can damage your health, mood, productivity, relationships, and overall quality of life. Chronic and long-term stress can be insidious, sneaky, and it creeps up on you over time. In the effort to be strong and forge ahead, we sometimes accept stress as a part of life, but the toll isn't noticeable until you break down.

One morning, as a single mother, while I prepared my children and myself for the day, I burst into tears. I remember, it was a Friday, and there was nothing particularly out of the ordinary about the day. It was the day stress reached its breaking point. I called around for someone to keep the children, but no one was available. Eventually, I managed to reach out to a retired acquaintance who cared for foster children, often juggling six to eight children at a time. "How do you do it?" I asked, clutching the phone to my ear in search of some magical answer. "Baby," she responded, "you are going to have to learn, all you can change, change. All else, FUCK IT." This advice has served me well when I am overwhelmed. I do not worry about things I cannot change at that moment. Table it until you can do something about it.

Long-term exposure to stress can lead to serious health problems. Chronic stress disrupts nearly every system in your body. It increases blood pressure, compromises your immune system, increases your risk of heart attack and stroke, contributes to infertility, and ages you before your time.

The symptoms of stress are: feeling overwhelmed, memory problems, poor concentration, poor judgment, pattern of negative thinking, anxious or racing thoughts, constant worrying, moodiness, irritability and agitation, the inability to relax, feeling hopeless, lonely, and isolated, and feeling depressed or generally unhappy. Symptoms can also include aches and pains, diarrhea or constipation, nausea, dizziness, chest pain, rapid heartbeat, loss of sex drive, frequent colds, eating more or less, sleeping too much or too little, procrastinating or neglecting responsibilities, and increased drug and alcohol use in an effort to relax. A lot of times, we set ourselves up for failure and stress ourselves out unnecessarily. We do not allow ourselves adequate time to complete tasks. We tell ourselves "I can get it done in half an hour," when we really need an hour.

I will say again and again, people are doing way too much in this fast-paced society, and there is a cost. It is killing us slowly. There is a reason preventable conditions such as hypertension, heart disease, and other preventable chronic conditions continue to be on the rise. Being strong is admirable, but sometimes the cost is too great.

STEPHANIE

I'm tired but can't sleep. I want to stop crying but can't. I'm exhausted but don't know how to relax. I have taken care of everyone around me for so long, I actually have no idea who I am. I have never seen Stephanie. I raised my three children solo and had to work hard to make sure my kids had everything that they needed. I thought it would all change and get easier once they were grown up, but then the grandchildren started coming. The stress from trying to save these fools I keep getting involved with, and helping my children and grandchildren in my life, has left me so tired. I keep one of my grandchildren during the day and work third shift. Right now I only get about two hours of sleep a day. I just can't do this anymore; I just can't go on like this. I crawl back to my dark hole, my bedroom, and cry for days. I get suicidal, but I can't kill myself because I can't think of a painless way to do it. If I shoot myself, that would hurt. If I take some pills, and I'm not successful in killing myself, and I'm laying up somewhere injured, that's painful. So I don't do it, but I have thoughts of killing myself every day. I want the pain to end. I can't even go to work. I can't sleep. I'm just empty. I hate myself and God. How much do you have to hate yourself to hate God?

When I was little my older cousin abused me sexually until I was 14 years old. He did things to me that no little girl should ever have to endure. Now in his 70s, I finally got the courage to confront him as an adult, and the bastard did not even remember what he did to me. Then my family took me away from my mommy, saying that she was unfit to raise me, so I went to live with my grandparents, and that was okay.

By that time, I was lost and confused and just wanted somebody to love me. Of course, I became rebellious and promiscuous, looking for someone to love me until the time my oldest daughter was born, when I was 25. Immediately after high school, I joined the Marines to get away from it all. I did two tours in Iraq, both in Fallujah. Man, I saw all kinds of stuff.

Life has always been intense for me. The military makes you grow up really quick, and after becoming pregnant I have been in serious and responsible mode since this time. Growing up without my mommy, I wanted to make sure I was there, a good mother to my children. To this day, I still don't know why they said my mom couldn't raise me. I always thought she was a good mom. I loved her, and I knew she loved me.

My family is not your "normal" family. A family is supposed to be loving and supportive – not mine. Outside of my grandparents, them motherfuckers is cut-throat and backstabbing. Jealousy and envy runs rampant. Talk about crabs in a barrel. Skin color and long hair caused a lot of problems for me coming up, from several relatives. Really, I didn't get it until my sister enlightened me in my 30s. To this day, I just know them motherfuckers hate my presence over some bullshit. I grew up with nothing but snide and sarcastic remarks about hair, skin color, and looks.

Several years back, while at a funeral one of my aunt's friends commented, "You're still pretty." You should have seen the look on my aunt's face. Guess what, I ain't mad at all. Dealing with my family just made me stronger. When your own family tries to slay you, people in the street ain't nothing. I give their asses the "light touch" and keep it moving. They know better than to say shit to me. Now all they do is stare at me. I guess I was supposed to fall, but I'm still standing.

The problem is I am my own worst enemy. I seem to be attracted to men who have a lot of problems, and I feel I need to fix them. I think it's because I need them to give me something to do. They keep my mind off my own demons. But all this is wearing me down, and it is just not worth it anymore. I don't know why Richard won't leave me alone. Left him for a reason. When he went to jail for rape and impregnated the woman, that was it for me. He is out of jail and just keeps stalking me. He just won't go away. I have put him out many times before and taken him back just as many, because he just has a way with words. He knows exactly what to say to get me to take him back. He is no good for me. Never has been.

The Mess

Stephanie suffered from depression and PTSD, residual side effects from her sexually and emotionally abusive childhood and from being in the Iraq war. She tries to bury herself in distractions, like the "projects," or men she becomes involved with, to avoid her demons. Stephanie neglects self-care in all four areas: sleep, leisure, exercise, and food.

Mindset

Focus on everyone but me. If I occupy my time by helping others, the demons will go away. I hate myself.

Miracle Question Response

I know the things I need to do. I want to finish school and volunteer somewhere. I need to start attending church regularly again. I would take better care of myself. It's time to stop letting my children run my life. I need to learn to celebrate more, to exercise, and celebrate all the small things. Essentially, it is time to stop talking and walk the walk. I know what I need to do.

Solution

As far as what is right in her life, Stephanie has her children and grandchildren and loves them. She has impeccable work skills, and her employer has been quite lenient when she calls off from work. Stephanie created her monsters by doing everything for her children, which has resulted in them being entitled and lazy. She also has an aunt who is a source of support. Most of all, I think she has resiliency and stamina. In spite of what she has been through, she is still standing.

Diagnosed with bipolar disorder – a diagnosis I never believed was accurate – Stephanie's issues appear to stem from running away from the ghosts of her childhood. She married a man 10 years her junior, and he used her, like most men she has been involved with in the past. She uses her "projects" and other vices, such as liquor and weed, as a distraction, but when life becomes overwhelming, she runs to the hospital to seek relief. She has been admitted to the psychiatric unit no less than 10 times in the last five years. The first time I treated her, she frequently missed appointments, but upon her return, she diligently maintained she was "serious this time." She was late for her first appointment because she could not find my new office. As I was leaving for the day, I found her in the lobby crying with red, tear-filled, weary eyes. From her seat, she looked up at me and said, "It is time to deal with the real Stephanie."

Stephanie looked different during these sessions. Her hair was natural and styled in a nice, neat little bun, and she did not have any makeup on. "If I'm going to try to find the real Stephanie, I have to take all that weave and makeup off," she said, smiling and glowing. It was probably the first time I really *saw* Stephanie, but there was still something bubbling beneath all the pain. During a subsequent session, she informed me that she wanted to leave the city, and I realized that she was planning to run away again. That was not the solution. She needed to learn to set boundaries. Helping others was fine, but not at the expense of her own sanity. She needed to confront her demons and be willing to do things for herself. She has, and she decided to postpone the move.

By the next session, Stephanie developed a game plan. She started being tougher on her children; they had ultimatums now. They had to take care of their own children. They had to get their own places because she was moving. She no longer wanted to be a people-pleaser. I asked her to write a letter to a friend that was going through the same thing she was going through and speak from the heart. Depressed and anxious individuals are, more often than not, overly critical of themselves but compassionate to the plights of others. The purpose of the letter was for her to start giving herself the same support and compassion she gave to others. As it just so happened, a real friend did later call her to vent about similar problems to those she was having, and as she spoke to her, she realized she was saying the things she needed to hear for herself.

Stephanie returned to journaling and completed her will. Penning one's thoughts often gives a sense of relief. Do you remember the diary you kept as a child? It was a place where you could write down all your secrets. One thing Stephanie found particularly difficult, though, was the assignment to write her obituary, and she has yet to complete this assignment. While it may seem morbid, the reality is that we are all born to die. The purpose of the exercise is to get you to realize that you will not live forever and that the time to work on your goals is now, and I believe she realized that in the end. Her next assignment was to develop SMART goals for the upcoming year, to give her life purpose and direction. SMART goals are detailed and are more likely to be realized because they are action oriented. Stephanie got into action. She confessed that there were times she wants to resort to old coping behaviors, and even admitted to inviting a new "project" into her home. When she saw the path she was headed down, she looked up at the guy and said, "Dude, you gotta go."

She has yet to start the SELF routine of adequate sleep, exercise, leisure, and nutritious food. We are not nocturnal animals and are born to sleep at night, so working nights and getting inadequate sleep only exacerbate Stephanie's issues, and she has no wherewithal or strength to solve her problems. This is really the first goal.

Stephanie continues to flip-flop between making progress and relapsing into her old ways of coping. She developed her SMART goals but has not taken any steps toward completing them. Stephanie knows what she should do and seems to always stop moving forward. We had a discussion about her being afraid to succeed. She agreed and stated, "I don't know why I hate myself." She continues to care for her grandchildren when she should be sleeping, although it is their mother who should be caring for them.

She now has new hurdles to jump through. Along with the depression, Stephanie previously suffered from PTSD. She was a Marine in the Iraq war. She is attempting to claim service-connected disability so she can be eligible for benefits. To do so requires her reliving the trauma she experienced in the war, including being left behind in a war zone by her fellow Marine. This has brought on the return of flashbacks, and she says she is realizing she did not come back the same. She says she previously compartmentalized this trauma and had been faring well.

Although she has trouble controlling her emotions, she states she no longer feels she wants to die. Stephanie states she is tired of being in defenseless situations. She was defenseless as a child when she was being molested, defenseless in the Marines when her fellow soldier left her behind, and defenseless in her job, and she is tired of it. So the goal is to learn how to defend herself. Currently she reports that she feels numb and the flashbacks are overwhelming at times. Luckily, she has her family to keep an eye on her. She still has fleeting suicidal thoughts and is less tearful. Now she realizes it is just life and is moving toward acceptance. Her primary diagnosis shifted from depression to PTSD as she attempts to claim service-connected disability so she can receive compensation.

We are still working to get her stabilized permanently.

"You are not required to set yourself on fire to keep others warm."
–Dr. Laura

LESLIE

I am forty years old, and I am a wreck. I can't sleep. I can't stop crying. I am completely exhausted. I just can't function, and I can't get through the day without having a panic attack. I hate my new job. No way did I expect it to be so draining emotionally. So much sadness and death. I'm so scared that I'm going to lose my job, because I'm calling in sick at least twice a week, but the panic attacks are so frequent that I can't do my job properly. Short-tempered and angry – that's me, and I keep on taking it out on my family. I feel so bad.

I just don't seem to care about myself any more. I am empty. I am completely empty. I never used to be like this. I was always a self-confident go-getter. There was nothing I couldn't conquer. I'm so tired and empty. Just empty. The more tired I get, the crankier I get. My family is getting affected. I don't mean to do this to them, but I'm just so tired. My husband has told me how he dreads coming home in the evening, because he doesn't know what to expect since my moods are constantly shifting. He doesn't know if I'm going to rip his head off when he walks in the door or if he will be well-received. The worst is when I realized how he and my kids mock me. They take bets on when I'm going to explode with rage next.

How can I not be angry? My husband spends all his money on himself and his video games. I'm the one who has to figure out how to pay all the bills. He had promised me that he was going to pay the electric bill and then didn't. When our electricity was cut off, he just looked at me with a look that said, "So what are you going to do about it?" He just doesn't seem to care.

I know the affair he is having with that woman online is only emotional. After all I have done for him, he has the nerve to fuck around on me. I'm so sick and tired of it – as if I don't have enough on my plate already. He never helps me around the house! He just doesn't seem to care! All he does is play his video games and meet up with his online bitch. Hell yeah, I call it like it is. I am so angry!

I am tired of having to stay strong. I have helped everyone in my family. They always run to me, but when I need help, there is no one. Some of them are happy I'm not doing well and are glad they have something to talk about. I've never been close to my brothers and sisters, and we drifted even further apart after my mom died. I'm so angry with her too. She just left me alone! Left me to deal with everything by myself. Didn't she know that she was the only one I had to turn to? The only stable and caring grown-up in my life.

I know that I'm right to be angry, that I'm right to be everything I am and feel everything I feel. I am always right. I don't care if that makes me end up alone. At least I'm prepared to stand up for what I believe in and never back down.

But then again, maybe I do need to change. I am on my third marriage, after all, and my previous husbands cheated on me as well. Maybe I'm the one pushing them away? Oh my God! I'm my mother! I am repeating her patterns! Maybe I do need to step back and look at my life more objectively. Maybe I do need to stop being so controlling and bossy.

The Mess

Leslie was tired of being the woman with the "S" on her chest but would not give up the need to control. It was normal for her to take on too much at work and at home, and having no one to turn to, she directed her anger toward her spouse and children. She also had residual PTSD from a childhood rape and a date rape.

Leslie's Mindset

If she does not do it, it will not be done properly. She is always right, and everyone should just go along with what she says. Her mindset is to conquer.

Miracle Question Response

I would be the kind of person my family wanted to be around and take on less stressful activities. Also, I would have a less stressful job.

Solution

Leslie has her family. This fulfills the need to belong and the need to have something, or someone, belong to us. Her go-getter attitude is a plus, but she just needs to learn how to balance it out with self-care and fun. The first goal was to get her to engage in self-care by getting adequate sleep, exercise, engaging in pleasurable activities, and eating a well-balanced diet. I suggested that she designate one day of the week to herself for engaging in whatever activity she wanted, helping her to cement "me time" as a regular thing. The second goal was to be proactive and not reactive. Take care of yourself before you burnout.

Leslie tried to get me to join in with her in the degradation of her husband at the start of her therapy, but she was the one who allowed this behavior and then tried to play the helpless victim. I suggested that, instead of arguing with her husband, she start setting some expectations and boundaries with him. Individuals tend to tune out a loved one yelling at them on a regular basis or become defensive and yell back because they feel attacked. If you yell all the time, there is no way for the other party to know what is serious, because everything is serious. By having clear expectations, they could agree on his responsibilities, which would make it easier to establish consequences. I also suggested she join a grief support group to process her emotions around her mother's death. Being around others struggling with, and overcoming, the same issues can be therapeutic. Lastly, I suggested she start doing nice things for herself on a regular basis to promote feelings of self-value and self-worth.

Leslie is a work in progress. She takes her medications regularly and is a little less reactive and explosive. She still struggles with the need to control. She notices that if she gives her husband the chance to figure things out, tension in the household is reduced. However, she has only been able to do this for short periods of time, and she reverts to her sharp tongue and control.

*"**People cry not because they're weak. It is because they've been strong for too long**."* –Author unknown

RICHARD

I am in my mid-sixties and completely miserable. I can safely say that I am not suicidal, but sometimes I wonder, at this late stage of my life, if I am actually better off dead. My wife never forgave me for cheating on her. Even though we are divorced, she still hasn't let it go, and I too have not let go. Recently I had a bad car accident, and my back has never been the same since. I seem to always be in pain. Back pain is the worst; it's always there no matter what you do.

I have thoughts of going to sleep and never waking up. I can't give up though. I can't die. My parents still need me. I know that they are independent financially, but they are not getting any younger. Who will drive them to the store for groceries when they are too old to see? Who will come round and fix the leaking faucet when my dad can't remember how? They still need me. I am responsible for them.

My back is so sore all the time that I can't keep my business going, my business that I worked my entire life to build so that I had something to leave behind for my children. I am such a failure, and I am too old to start again, too old to reach my goals and accomplishments. Everything is just falling apart at the seams, and it is all so hopeless. I just want to spend my days lying in bed. I have no motivation, and I am consumed by worry, and it paralyzes me.

In desperation for relief, I went on a three-day binge of painkillers and Southern Comfort. My children found me walking around in a stupor and called the doctor, who admitted me to hospital. I was only there for a few days, but it did help. While I was in hospital, I was so relaxed. I noticed I didn't have pain and didn't need meds. Maybe the pain is caused by stress. I'm stubborn, a little arrogant, but maybe I need to listen to the professionals.

The Mess

The depression from taking on too much and not enjoying life amplified as Richard tried to build a legacy. His sense of accomplishment centered on material things, which he had, and he lived in the past, agonizing over what went wrong in his marriage.

Richard's Mindset

He had to prove himself a success to his family. He felt like a failure in his marriage.

Miracle Question Response

I would have a legacy to pass down, and I would not have to do everything on my own. I also want to spend more time with my family. It would be really nice to have a companion of my own.

Solution

Richard has his family and still has his parents, who are in their 90s. This was a blessing in and of itself. He also has ingenuity and an entrepreneurial spirit. My experience with suicidal clients has been that most do not want to harm themselves; they simply want relief from pain and suffering. The body does not want to be in physical or emotional pain, and it will find a way to get relief eventually, either through either self-care or a psychological breakdown. This is why we need to pay attention to, and do something about, the alarms – fatigue, sadness, and excessive worry – our body and psychological states send to us.

Richard wanted to make money, and he was very adamant about this. There was no modifying this goal. I suggested he periodically take time out to enjoy life and the fruits of his labor and hard work. We clarified that it was *his* goal to leave a legacy to his family. None of his children expressed an interest or participated in his business.

Regarding the guilt from his failed marriage, I suggested he think seriously about what he wanted from his ex-wife. Did he want his ex-wife to return, forgive him, have a more amicable relationship, or what? Agonizing over her did not help, and it fed his depression. We also worked on reality acceptance. In reality, you have four choices: solve the problem, change how you feel about it, accept the issue as it is, or stay miserable. As for a companion, I suggested he work on becoming a man somebody would want to marry. Be the best you, a healthy you, so two emotionally and psychologically healthy people can come together. Andy Stanley has a podcast *New Rules for Sex and Dating* that is very helpful in this area. Richard went back to work full-steam ahead and has not since returned for therapy.

"Never get so busy making a living that you forget to make a life."
—Author unknown

LOW SELF-ESTEEM

"Esteem needs" is one of the five categories of hierarchal motivational needs that, as identified by American psychologist Abraham Maslow, make up an innate drive that helps us fulfill our desire to reach our full potential. Maslow posits that before we can reach our higher selves, or self-actualize, we must satisfy, or master, the lower physiological needs and needs of safety and security.

Esteem needs – the need for respect, self-confidence, acceptance, and to be valued or validated by others – are closely tied to the need to belong. Humans need to love and be loved, both sexually and non-sexually. This is why we join gangs, clubs, sororities and fraternities; volunteer; hang out in bars, sports, and cliques; and stay in good or bad relationships and dead-end jobs. These activities satisfy the need to belong and also the need for respect, recognition, fame, prestige, attention from others, strength, competence, mastery, self-confidence, and independence. It is even more important to love and nurture yourself when you are depressed or anxious and full of self-loathing. If you had a friend who was in such a situation, would you tell them to treat themselves the way you treat yourself? I doubt it. So why do you treat yourself like crap when you wouldn't even advise your worst enemy to treat themselves that way?

Low self-esteem is very common with depression and anxiety. Our self-esteem is at the core of the beliefs we have about ourselves, is what determines our self-worth, and is best understood by how it manifests itself. Low self-esteem is expressed when we are self-critical, self-blaming and self-doubting, and filtering out our positive qualities while focusing solely on our weaknesses. Other symptoms of low self-esteem are avoiding challenges and opportunities, being overly apologetic, and finding it difficult to stand up for oneself. It is being oversensitive, fearing disapproval, having an over-eagerness to please, and always putting the needs of others ahead of your own. It is feeling that rest and relaxation is undeserved and failing to indulge in self-care.

This intensifies feelings of sadness, guilt, shame, frustration and anger, leaving you physically tired and tense. The result is underperformance, rigidity, and having a fear of venturing out and making yourself vulnerable. In essence, self-esteem affects everyday life and what we think we deserve, and are worthy of, at any given moment.

EILEEN

My boss bullies me. She makes me feel so terrible about myself that I just want to kill myself. It put me in such a bad place that I ended up in the hospital, depressed and completely hopeless. I have been with that company for twenty years. I was a top-notch performer and my old boss's right-hand woman, but when he left and my new boss took over . . . she hates me. I don't know why, but she just seemed to. She started taking meaningful work away from me, making me do meaningless, redundant work. My coworkers alienate me and have been warned against talking to me. They are so scared that they will be treated the same way, so they have started avoiding me. When I confronted my new boss about it, she just yelled at me and told me to get the hell out of her office. My feelings were so hurt.

I just don't understand. I am scared of losing my job! How will I support my three children? I'm a good person! I treat everyone well, as I would expect them to treat me. I just don't know how to cope. I know my family is supportive, especially my mother. I still have my faith in God, but I just can't deal with my boss! I don't have the strength! I wish my ex-husband would be a little more supportive too. I know he is caring for our children while I try and get myself together, but I need him to be a little supportive of me. I guess that's a little silly of me though. How can I expect him to be supportive of me now when he has never been supportive? Whenever there was a problem, he would make sarcastic remarks such as, "Now that is what you are in therapy for, isn't it?"

The Mess

Eileen's depression stems from her acceptance of the role of helpless victim. It is also a naive expectation that others will treat her kindly because she treats them kindly and that everyone is fair and kind.

Eileen's Mindset

If I treat everyone right, everyone will treat me right.

Miracle Question Response

I would be able to go to work and not feel afraid.

Solution

She has a very supportive mother and a kind spirit. Eileen internalizes what others say, and this lowers her self-esteem. She does not consider that others may have malicious intentions that have more to do with their own insecurities and issues. Really, this says more about them than her. No one should depend on another for his or her value and self-worth, because giving someone that kind of power is dangerous. If someone has the power to determine your happiness, they have the power to take it away. Do you really want someone having this kind of power over you?

I suggested to Eileen that she radically accept her manager and quit living in a fantasy world where everything is fair and just. Radical acceptance means accepting a (non-life-threatening) situation for what it is, even if you do not approve of it or believe it to be okay. You take the information and cards you have been dealt, proceed wisely, and deal with the situation based on reality. Quit expecting people to play by the rules. An excellent book on this subject is Dr. Phil's *Life Code*. Dr. Phil discusses how to respond when you are playing by the rules and others are not.

After weeks of dreading a return to work, Eileen walked into therapy with her big-girl pants on and stated she was ready to face her boss. She applied the courage she had in other areas of her life to her work situation. She decided to fight back instead of being passive. No longer was she going to be the helpless, powerless victim. As suggested, she requested a meeting with her supervisor and the head of the company. Her plan was to present her experience and previous positive work history to the supervisor along with a documentation of events to support her claims. She stated she would like to remain with the company but not in the current hostile environment. She also requested severance pay and medical benefits along with the right to receive unemployment if she could not remain at the company. Eileen took her power back. Eileen did not return to therapy, so I assume everything worked out just fine.

"If I give them the power to feed me, I'm giving them the power to starve me." –Author unknown

DARLENE

I have tried to get my husband to go to couples therapy, and he finally agreed when I gave him an ultimatum but made it clear to me that he saw absolutely no point in it. When we got there, he took it as an opportunity to express how much he thought was wrong with me. He was very irritable and frustrated during the entire session. He outright said how he didn't find me attractive anymore, so much so that he had to use porn to get his rocks off. He made out as if everything was my fault and refused to take responsibility for anything that had gone wrong in our marriage.

I don't know what went wrong! When we first met, I was so attracted to this man. He was fun and adventurous. Now I wonder if he really was, or was I projecting what I wanted him to be and denying what he actually was? The truth is that I have not been happy with him for a long time, but I don't feel like starting over with someone else, and I don't want to be alone. This is my marriage. I don't know if I'll ever really find the right man for me. Right now, I really don't even want a man.

I know I am not easy to live with either, but I was not depressed or on edge or taking medication prior to meeting him. There is something wrong with all of us, but I know how to manage my crazies, and I don't neglect my responsibilities. I really want to take control of my life.

I have to make a change! I am determined not to reach the end of the New Year without having figured out what I want in life, and this means I have to make a decision about my marriage. I don't believe he is the one for me! And I really can't deal with his erratic behavior anymore! It keeps me on edge, not knowing when he may flip out or embarrass me in public.

If I leave, who will take care of him? Before, he had his parents, and they are deceased, and his siblings don't want to be bothered with him. I just don't know if I can continue living with him; he is so unpredictable. One minute he has a job and then the next he is fired because of his erratic behavior. One minute he agrees to see someone and the next he's refusing to admit that there is actually anything wrong with him.

I get so embarrassed when we go out because he is so critical and judgmental of everyone and everything around him. He is jealous of the attention I give my children, especially my sons. I am their mother; they need me too.

I just don't know anymore! He does the most unpredictable things! He has taken out several payday loans to have money to shop and gamble with. Right now he calls himself a professional real estate investor when he doesn't have the first clue of how real estate really works. He buys me expensive gifts that he cannot afford and expects me to not only cover the household expenses but also his payday loans. I have never dealt with anything like this before.

Note: I do not permit bashing during sessions. My goal in couples counseling is to have concerns shared in a diplomatic, respectful manner. Constantly hearing, "you did this" or "you didn't do this" is counterproductive to resolving issues, which can only be done through compromise and a mutual recognition of needs. Needless to say, Darlene's spouse liked neither my approach, nor my suggestion that he and Darlene seek individual counseling to work on their individual issues before seeking marital counseling. He became so angry, I was forced to stop the session and told him there was nothing I could do for them as a couple at this point. I highly suggested Darlene continue therapy on her own, and she did.

The Mess

Darlene's low self-esteem could be traced back to her childhood. She suffered from poor body and self-image issues and has no idea what makes her happy. Her spouse is bipolar, non-compliant, irritable, angry, and she fears he will one day be unreachable. She is not happy with him but feels he does not have anyone to care for him, and this makes her hesitant to leave. Because of her fear of being alone, she remains indecisive which keeps her in limbo.

Darlene's Mindset

The influence of a childhood where her mother discouraged her efforts to venture out made her habituated to staying in the safe zone and refusing to venture out when needed. Also, she does not challenge situations. She just goes along with things to keep the peace.

Miracle Question Response

If I were not dealing with depression, I would not have heaviness in my chest. I would not feel solely responsible for others. I would have inner peace and would feel comfortable with myself physically, emotionally, and mentally.

Solution

Darlene is just a sweet person. She is smart, attractive, and dedicated. She just has to see it within herself. Darlene thought her issue was her marriage when, in fact, it is her low self-esteem. She does have marital problems, but if she solved her esteem issues, she would discover the answers to her marital problems. Darlene does not feel attractive when, in fact, she is a very beautiful woman. She doesn't like her weight. She feels people are talking about her and laughing at her when she goes out in public. She has felt this way since she was a child. Clearly, her issues are self-esteem issues.

When I tried to get her to challenge some of her irrational beliefs, she commented that her parents taught her that you don't speak up for yourself, you just go along with the flow of things and do not cause trouble. Firstly, I wanted Darlene to realize she is not a child anymore. We all have childhood scripts. Some are good, and some are not so good. As adults, we have to learn to turn off the bad scripts and rewrite them.

Darlene and I decided to tackle the outer appearance first because this is the easiest thing to change. Changing the outside was to serve as a reminder that she was changing on the inside too. Every time someone commented on her outer appearance, she was to remind herself that she was changing on the inside too. The first thing I suggested to Darlene was that she get a professional makeover, which she did, and she looked even more beautiful. Next, she was to either accept her weight or do something about it by working out and eating better. Darlene started walking three times per week. She wanted to be comfortable with herself. She was to define in detail what this means, so she knows where to concentrate her efforts. Also the goal was to get her to focus on Darlene and what she wanted her life to look like, not so much on what was wrong with her marriage.

Darlene's mood improved. The depression lifted, but she was still anxious, mainly due to her indecisiveness regarding her marital situation. Her career was going very well, and her children were doing well, and this pleased her. The problem was just the tension in her marriage. She decided to stick it out until the end of the year. If, by that time, things have not improved with her husband, she plans to leave him. She struggles with letting go of her perception that she is responsible for him. I explained that she could still offer him support without remaining in an unhealthy marriage that is taking a toll on her. We discussed that her husband existed before she met him, and he will exist after her, although he no longer had his parents to bail him out when he got into trouble. Some couples are the best of friends after a divorce; they simply didn't make a good married couple.

Right now, indecision has left Darlene stagnant, and this contributes to her anxiety. I suggested that she stop arguing with her husband and allow the marriage to evolve on its own. Her intervening would only postpone the inevitable, which was yet to be determined. Again, I encouraged her to deal with reality and to make her decisions based on what he is doing now, not "if he would only do this or that." Most importantly, I advised her to determine how much she is willing to help her husband – whether she stays with him or not – and to stand firm once she reaches that decision.

Darlene started to get fed up with her husband's erratic behavior but still vacillates "if he does this, then she would stay." Although much of the discussion had been about her husband having no one, it surfaced that while Darlene had her children and family, it was she who feared being alone, as she did not have many friends. She uses her husband and his condition as a scapegoat to distract herself from dealing with her own issues and taking the steps to go out and find Darlene and what makes her happy.

Another task for Darlene is to develop a life outside of work and her family. I suggested she get comfortable with herself and start venturing out on her own instead of waiting around for others to go out before she starts living life. She is to then look for social activities to participate in so she can make friends. Just the thought of this brought on a great deal of anxiety for Darlene. It was recommended that she start by going to a coffee shop and having coffee with herself for at least 10 minutes. If she felt any anxiety, she was to stay there for 10 minutes, no matter what, and with whatever feelings arose and whatever else happened. She could do deep breathing exercises or use distraction to manage the anxiety.

At the coffee shop, Darlene felt scared, alone, anxious, and experienced a tightness in her chest. She was very uncomfortable and wanted to go home where she feels comfortable. This was all fueled by the irrational thoughts that people were talking about her and laughing at her. In her mind, the people in the coffee shop were saying something is wrong with her and wondering why she is alone. As a child, she felt people were laughing at her.

We processed her irrational thoughts using thought sheets. Thought sheets identify automatic thoughts that pop into our heads in stressful situations. You then identify the negative emotions that arise in response to the automatic or irrational thoughts. Next, you look for what proof you have that supports these thoughts. Almost always, there is no support. They are just irrational thoughts in your mind. Next, you come up with a more reasonable and rational response or thought. Darlene's irrational thought that people were talking about her made her feel anxious, sad, and fearful. Together we came up with more reasonable alternative thoughts that people had their own agendas and were not thinking about her. Maybe people did not notice her.

She countered that there are people who talk about others and say mean things about people. While this is true, I asked if she would say something mean to someone else, and she responded no. I asked why not. She responded, "Because it is mean, and I'm not a mean person." Mean people are insecure and have their own issues and intentionally seek out victims. There are people whose sole agenda each day is to make people feel bad so they can feel better about themselves. These are mean, sick individuals, and their intent has nothing to do with you. They know who to mess with and who not to mess with. Don't give off signals that reveal you are easy prey, even if you have to pretend that you are strong. This is when her large size and a stern look would go very far.

Thought sheets, and how to complete them, can be found online. It takes a little work to complete them in the beginning, but with practice, it will get easier. With practice, you will reach a point where you can do them quickly in your head.

Darlene still waivers as to whether she will stay in her marriage. Does she want to start her life over? No. Can she start over? Yes. Although she remains indecisive about her life's decisions, she does not want to turn 50 with the same problems. Her marriage is not the real issue. The real issue is her low self-esteem, and the main goal is to raise her self-esteem. She still has to decide how much she is willing to help her husband if she stays with him or leaves. I also suggested she give him some expectations with deadlines since he says he is changing his old, maladaptive behaviors. It is difficult to determine if his behavior is related to the mental illness and how much of his behavior is nurture or maladaptive, learned behavior. Stay or leave, if she continues to work on herself, she can come out a winner.

"Don't fear failure. Fear being in the exact same place next year as you are today." –Author unknown

HELENE

I am a tall, beautiful woman in my early forties. I am a dedicated mother of four children, a successful nurse, a supportive wife, but I am so depressed. It all started going downhill when my husband started having affairs. He even fathered an illegitimate child outside of our marriage. I became so lonely that I started my own affair, only to realize that the guy was attempting to just use me as a meal ticket.

During my husband and mine's last "let's work on our marriage" chat, I confessed to him about my affair. He went ballistic. That's when the emotional and verbal abuse increased and his mood swings became more extreme. One moment he can be loving and the next moment he is a raging lunatic. I continued to try for my children's sake. They are so young and need a family structure. So I would walk on eggshells around him. Sometimes, when he was in the middle of his rages, he would do damage to the house and tell the kids that it was my fault, that I was the cause of everyone's unhappiness.

The truth is that he had always had affairs. They first started shortly after we met, when we were still in college. I stayed with him because he convinced me that no one else wanted me. I think I went through the motions because this is what society expects you to do – go to college, get married and have kids. The problem is, I chose a man who has never fulfilled me, emotionally or sexually.

It is so important to me that my kids have a great childhood. Mine wasn't so great. My parents got divorced when I was very young, and my mother remarried an abusive man who was so mean to us. He was very strict and would often shame us. My mother would never stand up for us. I never felt like I fitted in. I was a mixed-race child in a mostly white town in the Midwest, and it was tough because I was too light for the African-American kids to accept me and too dark for the white kids to accept me. They used to tease me, call me "horse" because I was so tall. My cousin started it all; she used to tease and belittle me about everything.

While my childhood was not rosy, we did not go without the basics. My life is in stark contrast to my husband's childhood. He grew up in the inner city, and his mother was an addict who sold everything, including herself, to afford drugs. Basic necessities like food and clothing were scarce. He had to learn to hustle at an early age and briefly sold drugs to survive. His mother placed drugs and men on a pedestal and neglected her children – something my husband resents to this very day. He did not have contact with his father until the man received a terminal diagnosis for cancer. I do not doubt that he is jealous of my childhood and thinks I am privileged.

I so regret revealing my affair and wished things would go back to the way things were – those times were better than the present, but that's hardly saying much. My husband calls and texts my friends with lies about me, and they were so fed up with the harassment, they disassociated themselves from me. I'm embarrassed and isolated from friends and family, who live as far as three hours away. My family is not being aware of my struggles because I pretend everything is okay when I see them. I disclosed the truth about my marriage to a couple of family members, including my stepmother, and to my surprise everyone is supportive.

The Mess

Helene allowed her husband to erode her self-esteem, which had never recovered from negative messages she received as a child. She thought very lowly of herself, and this affected her perception of her physical appearance and positive qualities, which were many. Helene internalized the comments of others and allowed them to influence her thoughts and perceptions of herself, believing she was a bad person.

Helene's Mindset

Helene believed she was not worthy of better treatment and did not value her beauty, talents, attributes, and abilities. She didn't think she had the power to stop others from hurting her.

Miracle Question Response

Helene wanted life to go back to the way things were before she revealed her affair. Her self-esteem hadn't even crossed her mind until I suggested she learn to nurture and love herself.

Solution

Helene is also a kind person and self-sacrificing. I asked her if she would ever treat someone the way her friends, family, and husband treated her, and she emphatically responded no, yet somehow, she did not see that the malicious and evil things her friends, family, and husband did say more about them than they say about her.

Helene lived in a self-imposed prison. I recommended she venture out and reengage in the activities she had stopped participating in and reconnect with friends. Slowly, she reached out to old girlfriends, who were supportive and understanding. I suggested she get involved with the local chapter of her sorority and start attending homecoming events at her college. Her alma mater had a very strong alumni community, but she had never participated because her husband convinced her that no one from school liked her or had anything good to say about her. She feared old classmates would speak negatively about her, particularly about her former promiscuity that had stemmed from a need to be accepted. Of course, the only way to know would be to attend an event. I also suggested she engage more with her family.

My mother's sister, the one in the beginning of the book who told me to get out of grown folk's business, repeatedly told several other cousins and me when we were young children that our mothers weren't shit and that we weren't shit either. As a child, I knew something was wrong with this statement and situation. This is something you expect from an enemy in the street, not an aunt. God never allowed me to believe this statement, but to this day, whenever I see her, I can still hear her saying those mean-spirited words as if it were yesterday. I did not let her statement influence who I was but used it to fuel my drive and determination. This is some something Helene has to learn.

Helene started taking better care of her physical appearance and gained confidence around the house by successfully completing simple repairs — she was quite proud that she did not have to ask her husband. She started focusing on herself during sessions rather than on her husband, walked a little taller, and had a bounce in her step when she entered her office. She was brighter, and sessions became more upbeat and positive.

Sadly, her progress ended about a month later when she and her husband went on another one of their "let's work on our marriage" kicks and decided to see a therapist for marital counseling. When Helene walked into my office with her shoulders slumped and a monotonous voice again, I knew something was wrong. Their therapist had taken her husband's side on everything, leaving her confused and questioning her thoughts and the progress she had made. Everything we accomplished together was undone. She ended our sessions.

I called to check on her several months later, and though she said things were okay, I could hear the sadness in her voice. She was doing what she had always done. She was singing a song she did not want to keep singing.

"It's not what you are that is holding you back. It's what you think you are not." –Author unknown

TANYA

I am distraught and just confused. It feels like my life has been one big tragedy lately. My daughter's father, whom I have been with for seven years, is verbally, mentally and physically abusive. I can't believe I'm caught up in this situation. I'm scared to leave. He may try to kill me. I always thought, "No way would I let a man hit me." Dante had been in jail for dealing drugs, and I know what comes with this life. It can end with one police knock on the door. I have never had much, my entire life. Now I have a beautifully decorated 3000-square-foot home. Visitors come to my home and drop their mouths when they walked into my home. My daughter and I wear the best designer clothes and drive not one, but two luxury cars, a BMW M5 and a Corvette. I stay because I want for nothing, and I am quite comfortable in this lifestyle.

Before I met him I was independent, artistic, creative, and had an abundance of energy. I am a born-and-bred Empire girl from New York. I had a great, carefree life. I have been a model and a singer. Men adore me. I am the constant recipient of attention and affection from men from all kinds of backgrounds. When I first met Dante, he was so fun and wonderful. We shared our hopes and dreams. He made me feel that my dreams and aspirations were possible, that anything was possible. We were going to build a fabulous empire and life together. In the beginning, I didn't mind that he was controlling. I actually thought it was cute and found it flattering. Then one day, it just didn't seem so cute anymore. The beatings started occurring more frequently, and I walked on eggshells, trying to avoid triggering his anger.

My family cannot visit, because Dante controls my every move. Even when he was in prison, he had people watching me. My family begged me to leave him. They tell me I have changed, that he has taken away the bubbly girl they once knew and loved. But I still stay with him because I love him. He tries to manipulate my parents and has convinced them that the problems in our relationship are my fault.

The only thing stable in my life is church, but I stopped going. I have stopped everything – church, exercising – I only get a couple hours of sleep because of the worry about everything.

When I was 15, I had a gun held to my head when my parents' home was robbed. The guy put a 9 millimeter to my head and tied my parents and my siblings up in the basement for over 24 hours. I kept saying to myself, "This is it. I'm about to die."

The next year, my first love was killed in a robbery while walking down the street. We were supposed to hook up, and I cancelled on him. If we would have hooked up, I know this would have prevented his death. I have lost a lot people close to me. Between the PTSD, the trauma, and the guilt, some days I just don't know how to cope. Weed is the only thing that seems to help, even if temporarily.

One day I finally found the courage to leave Dante. I couldn't take the beatings anymore. He begs and pleads, blows up my phone and stalks me. He took my daughter for a week. How could he take my baby away from me? I was so scared, so helpless. He couldn't handle the responsibility of a four-year-old and returned her. I don't know why I am always attracted to men in the fast life. How can I be so committed to a bad relationship but cannot commit to finishing anything that is going to benefit me?

Well, Dante got picked up again. He is facing hard time based on his previous history. Now I am concerned about my daughter growing up without a father. It feels like everything is surreal. Dante wants to marry me. I'm doing everything to help him, but I do not have any emotional attachment to him. I do not care about him the way I use to.

The Mess

Tanya felt that she had no control over her life when, in reality, she was giving up her power. She had stopped using the common sense God gave her, choosing to live in a fantasy world with her daughter's father, and she felt she had to have a man by her side, no matter the situation.

Tanya's Mindset

Tanya liked the action, drama, and excitement that came from the type of life she lived and the people she associated with.

Miracle Question Response

Without my depression, I would be happy, expressing my creativity. I wanted desperately to get back to my old, confident self. I would finish what I started.

Solution

Tanya has a lot of energy and creativity and is dedicated to helping others. One of her counseling goals was to find her own peace of mind, though she could not initially define what that meant. She considered moving down South. However, if you take the same old you to someplace new, old problems are sure to follow.

I had her complete a life-balance wheel. She picked her career as the first aspect to work on, as she had always been a jack of-all-trades but master of none. Because her happiness tied into expressing her creativity, she wanted to channel her creative energy into fashion design by making and selling clothes. She also realized she wanted to return to school and give back by volunteering. In addition to the life-balance wheel, I had her complete her obituary. When it is time to depart this world, it's simply time to go. I have seen people at the end of their lives, in despair, leaving behind nothing but regrets. I have seen others say, "I am okay with death. I lived a good life." What do you want said about you at the end of your life?

One session, I could see it in her face. I said, "I know you are not thinking about getting back with your daughter's father." It is quite common after breakups to return to what is familiar, even when we know it is not a good move. Loneliness and wanting to be held makes us forget why we left certain people in the first place. The couple of dates she went on were disasters

We are quickly reminded, when we return to an ex, why we left. She admitted that she was thinking of returning to her daughter's father. I explained to Tanya that we, as humans, are born to relate, and we want to be with others, and there is nothing wrong with wanting to be with someone, but we have to be selective about whom we choose. She eventually came around and realized she did not need to be in a relationship at this time. Instead, she needed to get herself together.

Tanya is still dealing with the pull of her daughter's father to drag her back into a relationship. He wants to get married. Right now, she is not acquiescing to this proposal and wants no part of him. She is sad her daughter will not grow up with her father. She says she wants to break free completely but remains connected with him, beyond him being the father of her daughter. Things were going fine until he got busted for selling drugs again and is facing hard time. It's all so surreal right now. All the material things she was concerned about are gone, and she questions whether it was all worth it. She feels the need to be there for him and to be supportive. She is living with her parents, has a new job, plans to enroll in college, and is linked with a domestic violence support group. With a content smile, she says, "I'm strong again."

"The great thing about life, when you feel you have gone off track you can always get back on track. Change your mind. Change your life."
–A Different Approach

FAMILY PROBLEMS

Family issues can encompass all of the emotions – joy, sadness, anger, fear, trust, disgust, disappointment, joy, and pain. When it's good, it's good, but when it's bad, it's *bad*. Families are supposed to love and protect and provide a sense of identity. This is not always the case. Sometimes you can get more love and support from a total stranger than from your own family. Parents can lead you down the right path, or they can screw you up for a lifetime. Siblings can be like two peas in a pod, or there can be enough hate, jealousy, and envy to carve irreparable distance. We cannot choose our family members, but we can choose how we deal with them.

There are no easy answers for family issues, but sometimes, understanding events that have occurred in their peoples' can provide some understanding of their behavior. A client now understands why her father treated her badly; she was the product of her mother's rape. My maternal grandmother was not very nurturing until my adult years. I later found out that her mother passed when she was two, she had a mean stepmother, and that led to her being homeless and on her own at age fourteen. While playing with one of her great grandchildren, she stated out of the blue, "I didn't know nothing about raising no children." This instantly changed my perception of her. Perhaps healing can occur when we accept family members as they are and not what we need them to be.

With that said, this does not mean you are to take any mess from your family. Boundaries must be set, firmly establishing what you will, and will not, tolerate. Make of list and place each family member in a category of supportive or non-supportive. The ones who are on the non-supportive list, accept them for who they are, give them the light touch and deal with them with a long-handled spoon. Only you can determine the amount of hurt you are willing to endure. Make it known what you are willing to put up with. Do not waiver, and the rest is up to the other parties.

MICHAEL

I'm in my early seventies and have been diagnosed as bipolar disorder, mixed. I swing from very happy to very sad in the space of mere minutes. Some days, I am afraid to leave the house and on others, I have these grand delusions and buy things I can't afford. I just need someone to talk to when I am in these spaces. It really helps to talk to someone.

There was a time when I had lots of money. I lived a great life of extravagance, collected fine art pieces and books, wore only the finest clothes, surrounded myself with wealthy people, and donated lots of my money to the arts. Now I am always sick, and I have nothing left but my art collection that I love. I live in a crappy, drug infested, and crime-ridden neighborhood, a far cry from my heyday. I was an alcoholic, and the money left faster than I earned it.

My depression is worse over the holidays because I have no money for Christmas. For the first time in my life, I had to rely on donations from hunger centers. I used to love the holidays. I miss my mom's homemade mince pie! I actually managed to get all the ingredients but was too sick to make it on Christmas day.

I am so scared to drive, and I hate having to rely on other people to take me places; it's so degrading. I really wish I could drive again so that I can be independent and get out more on my own and go when I want to.

My health is in a terrible state. I am deaf in both ears, and only one of my hearing aids actually works. The machine they put in my back to help stop my uncontrollably pissing on myself does not work, so I frequently wet the bed and have to wear adult diapers. This makes me feel even more like crap. I have had multiple strokes and seizures and have numbness on my left side. I fall on a regular basis, and I hate using this damn walker.

I am so frustrated trying to access the services that are supposed to help me, and the frustration of it just makes me even more depressed. I know it is because I'm gay. The health aids they send to help me steal from me, and those shitty dinners from Meals on Wheels they send don't even fill me up.

But I'm not worried about myself. I'm worried about George, my partner. Our families rejected us because we are gay. They refuse to see us and have totally cast us both out. I have tried to teach George how to pay the bills and do the grocery shopping, but I really can't help but worry who will care for him when my body finally gives up on me and I'm gone.

We really need to talk about what happened to me as a child. I wonder if I am gay because a teacher sexually abused me. My father physically abused me. He would just beat me until I was black and blue all over. We lived on a farm in Pennsylvania.

One day I was working in the loft. For no reason, my father came up, grabbed me, and tossed me over the loft. Another time he took a cattle prod and kept poking me in the genitals. By the time I got to the house he must have told my mother because she had called the doctor. The doctor told them if something like this happened again, he would call the authorities. This did not stop the abuse; they just did not call the doctor. Sometimes I would hide high up in the trees, hoping to avoid my father. I would run home and do my chores as fast as I could, but sometimes he would come home early, and I would be beaten.

The Mess

The depression and isolation from family and the difficulty accessing resources. Trying to figure out why he is gay. The PTSD from the sexual and physical abuse.

Michael's Mindset

He believes his problem of receiving the run-around when trying to access services is due to his sexuality. He must maintain the façade that he still has money.

Miracle Question Response

I would be able to get out more and drive a car again. I would also move to California near George's sister, who has been supportive of our relationship and could take care of George.

Solution

Michael is very trusting and a self-taught, very well-read and intelligent man. Michael has stopped wasting time with social service agencies that fail to provide services he is eligible to receive. He is learning to ask to speak with supervisors and write letters to directors, and this has been a great help. He is quite proud of this accomplishment and is less depressed. To get some pleasure back into his life but not get into debt from overspending, he is allowed to research items he would like to purchase and make one small online purchase per week. He has yet to inquire about the public transportation available for the handicapped that would enable him to get around more, but it is on his list. I also suggested he speak with his partner's sister to see if she is willing to take on the responsibility of looking after his partner when he is no longer around.

Unfortunately, Michael is now showing signs of dementia but is still able to live independently with the help of home health aides and his partner. Before further decompensation occurs, I plan to instruct him to ask someone to assist him in driving one last time. Perhaps a driving instructor with a brake on the passenger's side, in case something happens. He also struggles with his own mortality, as many of his friends are passing. The reality is, we are all born to die. All we can do is live the fullest life possible with the resources we have.

"You cannot get out of life alive, so you may as well have a good time."
–Les Brown

MELINDA

I'm depressed and frustrated, but I know God will make a way. He always does. I know I am in my thirties now and cannot keep making the same mistakes. Raising three children on my own is hard, but my kids are my world. I go without so they can have the things they need. I try to make up for what their fathers do not do and what I did not have while growing up with parents who were addicted to drugs.

Right now I am financially strapped. I'm behind on everything, my rent and my car note. The children always need, and I just don't have enough money coming in right now. I hate that I yell at them so much. Money is tight. If I get a part-time job, I'll end up paying a babysitter. I am damned if I do and damned if I don't.

I'm so pissed off at their fathers. They think that all they have to do is buy a toy here, and a pair of shoes there, and that makes them good fathers. They don't give me any help, but when they do show up, they are dressed in designer clothes and the latest athletic shoes, and flashy jewelry, and nice cars. None of them help with day-to-day care. Only my youngest son's father is supportive emotionally and spends time with our son on a regular basis.

My family helps me out a little, my dad, my fourth stepmother, my grandmothers, and my aunts. I would describe my childhood as fucked up. Both of my parents were on drugs and ran the streets. At age 10, my father got clean and I went to live with him and his new his new wife who was physically and emotionally abusive, while my father worked two jobs and ran the streets. I bullied other kids in school because I was angry. I didn't have my mother. All I wanted was to be loved and cared for, for someone to understand me.

I still only see my mother once in a while. She is still on drugs and on the streets. My father says mean, sarcastic things to me, and I have to beg him to provide and keep his own grandchildren. Yes, I am pissed off with my dad for letting that bitch that he married do what she did to me. Yes, I really feel like he could step up, make it up to me and help me with my children from time to time. After all, they are his fucking grandkids.

I do have hopes and dreams. I want to start my own cleaning business or open up a cleaning business. I want to go back to school and get a degree in business management.

The Mess

Depression and the displaced anger. Looking for men to give her the love she so desperately wants. Trying to force people to do what she wants them to do. Living in a world of ifs. If only her parents were not on drugs, her life would be so much different. If only she had help. Poor decision making and looking for someone to guide her and give her what she did not get in childhood.

Mindset

Melinda believes that others, namely her family, should help her because she is struggling. She thinks others should help her out of the holes she digs with poor choices and decisions. She believes she is entitled.

Miracle Question Response

My mother would not be on drugs, and my father would help me with the care of my children. My father would help care for the children and buy them the things they need. We would have more family activities together, like Sunday dinner and family outings. I would also finish school and open my own cleaning business.

Solution

She is naive and caring. She is an excellent mom. First, it was suggested she decide what she wants to accomplish in life for herself and her children. Melinda was scattered, jumping from one idea to the next and not completing anything. She was to stop expecting her family and friends to jump on whatever get rich scheme she was into and stop being disappointed and angry when they did not. I recommended she first learn to manage what she currently has going on before taking on more. If she could not manage the demands she has on her time now, surely she could not manage any more. If the universe gave her more, she would most likely mismanage that also. This is why most lottery winners are broke within a year. They did not know how to manage a little money; they were given more and mismanaged that too. Melinda was to also have a conversation with herself and consider exactly what she wanted from her father. She was to then sit down and talk with her father and discuss how she feels and what she wants from him. It would then be his choice to acquiesce or not, at which point she had to make some decisions based on his response and actions. We discussed how it is hard enough keeping ourselves together and that we have no right to go around telling others what they should do, especially when we are not together. It was recommended that she learn to accept people as they are and not for what she needed them to be. This included her children's fathers, her father, and her mother.

During one session, we had a "come-to-Jesus" moment, a moment in which the truth about her need to change was realized, and she was not too happy with it. "The truth hurts" is not just a saying. People would rather hear a lie, distort reality, and live a lie than deal with the truth. Again, reality acceptance was in order. The children were hers.

The bottom line is, no one was responsible for those children but her and their fathers. Reproduction 101: If you lie down and have sex, you may procreate. She was the one who decided to have intercourse and created those children for whatever reason. She was the one who selected their fathers. If they were shit, oh well. She picked not one of them, but three, of the same type of man. She was to stop having more expectations for them than they had for themselves and focus on getting herself together. Yes, it would be nice if her family helped more, and it would be nice if her kids' fathers helped, but no one was obligated to help care for the children but her. She was to consider that her family had their own lives and struggles and to quit drawing them into hers.

Cursing out the fathers of her children, her father, and her family did not get her anywhere, and it was advised that she stop this. People are more likely to help if you show you are helping yourself and you have other options. She was instructed to ask one time for what she or the children needed and move on. If there were no results, she was to look to other avenues to get what she needed or do without.

Next, she was to start cleaning up life's messes she had created due to poor decisions, whether it was her bad credit or the many people she owed money to, and stop blaming and making excuses. Melinda obviously wanted and needed guidance. Seeking guidance should be done with caution. There is a difference between seeking guidance and wanting others to think for you. Be very, very careful from whom you seek guidance. It is wise to seek guidance from individuals who make smart decisions, not individuals who talk about being wise or can tell you what to do but their own lives are hot messes. Look to individuals who possess integrity and who have the ability to think logically and critically. If they have actually accomplished what they are trying to accomplish, they should be able to give some advice to make your road less bumpy. Most importantly, seek advice from someone who wants you to succeed.

Understand that the majority of your family members and friends cannot tell you to go for it or to shoot for the moon when most cannot think outside the box regarding themselves, let alone you. Be careful who you share your thoughts and ideas with, because some people are waiting for the opportunity to belittle you or cut you down because of their own insecurities and shortcomings. Individuals on the receiving end typically internalize what others say, not realizing that what people say and do says more about them than it says about you.

Guidance can come from many sources. Be open. At times, it seems that those closest to us offer the least support. Not only are they not going to support us, they will go out of their way to try to set up roadblocks and obstacles. Sometimes the most poisonous venom comes from friends and family. This is painful to accept. Acknowledge the hurt, and keep it moving at the same time. Be open to guidance coming from people you don't know. Total strangers can sometimes offer a world of wisdom. I suggested that Melinda lay low for a while until she starts making progress and getting the right people in her life. She really needed a different circle of friends, most of whom are in the same boat and have the same mindset as her. Next, I suggested she have regular "me time" away from the children. Not taking a break from your children can drive you crazy. Taking time for yourself allows you to reset.

She has yet to complete the writing assignment, "What would your four-year-old self tell the adult you today?" I posed this question in order to get to the bottom of exactly what she was trying to explore emotionally. Sometimes when we experience extreme stress or traumatic events, we continue to grow chronologically and physically, but psychologically we are stymied and are basically stuck at the stage we were in when the trauma occurred. Melinda is a work in progress. She struggles with the new insights she is learning in therapy and is reluctant to give up old behaviors.

"No one is coming to save you. This life of yours is 100% your responsibility." –Author unknown

NANCY

I come from a very abusive background. I was verbally and physically abused by my mother and my father. No matter what I did to try to make my parents happy, it never seemed to be enough. I was forced to stay in the house, away from others as a child. For reasons unknown, my parents treated my sisters better. My uncle told me that my siblings and I had come along at a bad time; my father felt trapped by my mother and began to mentally, physically, and emotionally abuse my mother. Both of my parents were very unhappy with each other.

It hurts me that my family does not come around to see how I am doing. I try to reach out and be involved with them and their lives, but they reject me. I crave interaction with my youngest brother and sister. We were close prior to my mother's death and before they got on drugs several years ago.

What made me decide to get counseling is Thanksgiving Day. I was worried about some pending results from a CAT scan of the brain. I did not want ruin my children's Thanksgiving, so I kept it secret from them.

I called my on-and-off, long-term beau on Thanksgiving crying, expecting him to be caring and just listen to my worries, but instead he told me that he is not my therapist and not responsible for my happiness. I could not believe it and burst into a flood of tears. There was no compassion, no support, and no soothing. I was shocked and very upset by his response. I just became distraught and further depressed.

The Mess

Nancy is disappointed in the failure of others to behave and respond as she expects them to. Nancy's belief is that family should be involved with each other. She is emotionally needy, and this seems to turn people off.

Nancy's Mindset

She believes she ought to be treated exactly as she treats everyone else.

Miracle Question Response

There would be more communication, interaction, and support from my family.

Solution

She, too, has a kind and caring heart. Nancy has the love of her children. Nancy needed to understand that people are free to respond as they choose. As it related to her boyfriend, one explanation was that he was simply an asshole. Another was that, overall, men are inherently problem-solvers, and if they cannot do something about a situation, they feel useless and, therefore, retreat. Nancy agreed that she could not change him, but she could change the way she processed, managed, and responded to the situation. I was proud that she gained insight into her patterns and recognized her tendency to get hurt when people failed to meet her expectations.

I asked if there were qualities she liked about him. While he did have positive attributes, she concluded and accepted that he could not give her what she needed, which was compassion. I suggested that Nancy focus on what she did have – five beautiful children who loved and were concerned about her. When she revealed to her children her health concerns she had hidden from them over Thanksgiving, they offered the compassion and support she needed, and they were only upset that she had not told them sooner.

Regarding her siblings, we agreed that she could extend the type of relationship she would like to have, but their reciprocation was not up to her. For Nancy, relationships and being there for others in times of need is very important, and there is no need to apologize for that. She is learning to accept the choices of others and appreciate the loving relationships she already has. Nancy has decided it is best to give the spaces in her heart to those who are willing to work for them and now focuses on getting herself together.

Now instead of moping, she said she is glad her ex is gone. She now believes what she sees about him and states she could not breathe with him because he was so suffocating. She states she had to suffer to learn the lesson. Smiling, she reflected, "This is where I am now. It seems like I get disappointed when I have expectations from others and they don't meet them. It hurts me so bad my head hurts." Letting people into her heart, caring too much about others, and wanting others to be okay, all while she goes through her pain and cannot count on anyone, hurts her so.

Holding on to what is supposed to leave us blocks us from future blessings. Within a short time of releasing the guy she broke up with, a male acquaintance she has known for several years invited her to dinner. Reluctant, she said, "What the hell?" and went over to his house. When she pulled up, this gentleman was waiting at the end of the driveway for her to arrive. They had dinner and just sat and talked for hours. He asked about her health and her children. Eventually she took a shower, and he asked if he could wash her back, and she acquiesced. With a great big smile of satisfaction, she said this was the first time any man had washed her back and it felt good. There was no sex, they had an enjoyable evening, and she later went home.

Regarding her family, even Stevie Wonder could see that Nancy's siblings were being intentionally malicious toward her. They did not invite her to family events. She was okay with this, whereas before it made her sad. We discussed that this is just hateful and mean, and it said more about their character and intentions than it said about her.

In the beginning, she was mad and crying about the things in her life, but she is now thankful for the lessons and says she is ready to receive God's blessings. She talks to God more and does not cry anymore. "The devastating part is over," she said. She realizes that she needs to keep experiencing the consequences of her life choices because she did not learn the lessons.

She completed the life balance wheel and has several dips in several areas. Health and wellness is the first area she would like to tackle. Her goal is to lose 25 pounds by spring. She wrote the steps that she needs in order to accomplish this, so it is not a pipe dream. She plans to exercise

3 times per week, to stop downing herself, to allow no one to stop her, and to eat better.

She is guided by the affirmation that God is the center of her life now and she has peace. In her soft spoken, sweet voice she says she is learning to accept people as they are. After having some sit-down time with herself, she decided to no longer be in denial and to stop blaming people for hurting her. She is learning to accept people the way they are and summed it up by saying, "I don't have to be around them."

You will end up disappointed if you go through life thinking people will do for you as you do for them. Not everyone has the same hearts."
–Author unknown

HEALTH ISSUES

If you have your health, you are rich beyond measure. Being mentally and physically sound is the most valuable thing you can have. In my professional capacity, I have watched many people die; therefore, I have seen people who would give anything to have health and vitality again. Most of us take our health for granted until it becomes impaired.

GIGI

When I was in my thirties, I was in a really bad car accident that left me with a debilitating back injury and crushed ankles. I just can't take the stress of any more operations, even though I am still in a lot of pain. My injuries have made it impossible to continue my job as a nurse, which has made it really difficult to care for my five-year-old son.

My anxiety attacks are so bad that I have to totally stop what I am doing when they happen. Even with the breathing techniques that my therapist gave me, I still have trouble calming down after an episode. Then my back pain kicks in, and I have to keep on standing up and repositioning myself to relieve it. I am on oxycodone, but I am so scared that I will get addicted to it, so I take it only when it is really, really necessary. I smoke pot because it helps with the pain. It seems to be the only thing that helps, but I cannot take the risk of testing positive by my doctor. I now have to rely on welfare, food stamps, and the help of my family to get by. Social Security has denied my applications twice. I really am so scared about being able to take care of my son properly. I really want to work but cannot due to the chronic pain.

It's so hard to accept that I have lost my physical and financial independence. I used to be able to work double shifts at the hospital with no problems. I could afford a nice place. I had a nice car, and I could provide everything that my son needed and wanted. Now I am reduced to days of constant pain and peeing in my pants all the time because of my incontinence. I have to wear diapers, but I hate wearing them. Every time I go out, I am afraid of the embarrassment of wetting myself in public. Even though my family is supportive, I really hate staying with my sister. She is just "nasty." She's so untidy and has absolutely no personal hygiene. It really upsets me because how am I supposed to do all the house cleaning by myself in my condition? Even though I try really hard to remain positive, some days I just want to give up.

The Mess

Gigi battled anxiety and depression in the wake of her accident because she could not accept her loss of independence.

Gigi's Mindset

She focused entirely on what she could not do and what she used to be able to do.

Miracle Question Response

I want to be free of pain and regain my independence.

Solution

She has a very supportive family. Reality acceptance was Gigi's biggest issue in the aftermath of the accident. Clients who must master reality acceptance have four options: stay miserable, solve the problem, change how they feel about it, or accept it. The truth was that Gigi would never be able to return to her prior functioning and instead needed to focus on what she was capable of doing. On her better days, she can use her walker and clean the house. I encouraged her to take her son to the park. Even if she could only sit and watch him play, they were still spending quality time together, which is all her son ever wanted.

I also suggested she start a gratitude journal by counting her blessings, which included her caring, supportive family. Gigi learned to accept that her sister had a right to keep her household in whatever manner she saw fit, and eventually, her sister's housekeeping skills improved a little bit. Gigi dropped out of therapy due to insurance problems. Periodically, I call to check on her. She stated that she still has good and bad days but is dealing with her condition.

"When we meet real tragedy in life, we can react in two ways – either by losing hope and falling into self-destructive habits, or by using the challenge to find our inner strength. Thanks to Buddha, I have been able to take this second way." – Dalai Lama

DIANE

I am depressed about my marriage because my husband is unsupportive. I have been out of work for several months due to multiple back surgeries after falling on some stairs that resulted in difficulty walking and extreme pain. I can no longer work in the automobile factory where I have worked for 17 years because it involves walking and standing. What am I supposed to do? I have three young children to take care of, one of whom has special needs. I hate the fact that I cannot move about as I please, and most of my days are filled with pain. I'm depressed that I no longer can drive because my legs unexpectedly give up on me. To cope, I drank more and would just lie in bed all day after sending the children to school. I decided to stop drinking and went to rehab for 30 days and became involved in AA.

Not only does my husband make excuses as to why he could not take me to my AA meetings, he intentionally brings liquor into our home, knowing I'm in recovery. While at a social function for my husband's employer, I came close to losing my sobriety because liquor was present and my husband was drunk.

Now that I am totally dependent on him, he developed a cocky attitude. We have arguments all the time; sometimes it is because of my big mouth. I don't hold my tongue. But now I have to and agree to whatever he wants. I have never had to do this my entire life.

Out of all of this, though, my greatest fear was "losing my pretty." I fear I will no longer be attractive in my husband's eyes. The weight gain and use of a walker and cane make me feel unattractive.

Growing up, my parents were crack addicts. Now, they try to make up for their past by buying things. I declared there was nothing my parents could give me that would erase what happened. I had to go without the latest fashions and so forth and was the subject of being teased by other children until high school, when I learned how to hustle. Looking good is very important to me. I do not leave the house without being well-dressed. I love to shop. If I have an extra dollar, I'm going to spend it. I make sure my children have designer clothes and that they want for nothing, even though my husband and I agree it is making the children greedy and unappreciative.

The Mess

Diane's issues not only stem from her marriage and health, but also her childhood. She has a lot of unresolved anger from these three things.

Diane's Mindset

Diane covered her problems by shopping for beautiful things. If she dressed pretty enough, her husband would pay more attention to her. She is also trying to avoid any reminders of her upbringing.

Miracle Question Response

I would not be so angry all the time and would communicate with my family better. Specifically, my husband would pay more attention to me.

Solution

Diane has survivor qualities. She is a hustler. I suggested Diane stop arguing with her husband and instead think strategically about how to get what she wanted. When she did ask him to do something, she needed to be concise and detailed instead of expecting him to read her mind. In response, her husband became a little kinder. She was ecstatic when they went out on a date that he initiated and he carried her when she could not walk. This made her feel treasured.

Diane had to face the reality of her health situation and focus more on what she could do instead of what she couldn't. She began developing business ideas that would allow flexibility for good days and the ability stay home on the bad ones. A benefit of being at home was having the time to care personally for her special-needs son, allowing him to forego multiple hospital stays.

She stopped arguing with her husband and found he became more helpful. She is looking for a new career to accommodate her physical limitations and is still sober and more optimistic.

"I'm a survivor of life. I try to give the glory to God and appreciate what's happening to me." –Mike Epps

ANISHA

I am depressed for several reasons. I was taking too much medication for my lupus and fibromyalgia. I had to take pain medication to function. I literally went crazy. I struggle to complete daily activities, and movement is getting worse due to my fibromyalgia. For years, I have taken medication and pushed past pain in order to function and take care of my children. While on short-term disability, I was let go from my job as an accountant. I've worked hard all of my life, often holding two or three jobs at a time to provide for my children. To sacrifice and give up a very successful career to end up literally destitute is unbelievable and too much for anyone to bear. I really want to work but can't. Without any income, I missed a mortgage payment for the first time ever. My home is facing foreclosure, and I am behind on every bill. There are no programs to help me besides food stamps and medical.

Even though none of my family members have ever been supportive, I was disheartened that several family members are glad to see me struggle. Although I'm not shocked, it does hurt that instead of being supportive and asking if I need anything, they are running around gossiping and hoping I fall completely on my face. They really don't know what is actually going on and make up stuff so they can have something to talk about. So much for blood.

The Mess

Anisha spent an excessive amount of time questioning other people's actions and letting them affect her mood, accepting what they dished out to prevent contention. She could not accept the reality, like how her employer had let her go even though she was an exemplary worker, or that she was extremely conscious of the weight she gained as a side effect of her medications but was not doing anything about it. She became frustrated that she had served her country by joining the Air Force, worked hard and raised her children without any assistance, and now has to beg and constantly jump through hoops in an effort to try to get Social Security disability when there are people who get it and nothing is wrong with them.

Anisha's Mindset

Anisha believed in playing by the rules. She was fair, expected others to be fair as well, and was disillusioned when the world did not adhere to these morals as carefully as she did.

Miracle Question Response

My ultimate wish is to be able to work again. I realize I have to do something different. Right now I just want to live the best life I can.

Solution

Anisha is a fair and just person. She wants to see the good in everyone. Anisha needed to learn to stop dwelling on others, become more comfortable with herself, and stay focused. Slowly, she began to accept her medical condition and planned to appeal her Social Security denial. I suggested that in the meantime she strongly consider opportunities that she could still take advantage of in her field. At this point, she had focused too heavily on the past that she'd loved, instead of moving on and considering other areas, like teaching.

Because she was unhappy with her weight, I encouraged her to start some moderate exercise to get the weight off and to improve her mood and anxiety. She took up hiking and saw great improvements. Because money was a factor, she felt limited in her options for leisure, and we came up with some free activities she could engage in, such as taking classes at a neighborhood community center.

Practicing acts of kindness and compassion can boost your mood. (Dr. Fred Luskin of Stanford University has several lectures on happiness and compassion that are worth checking out on YouTube). Anisha realized that she wanted to do something for the less fortunate, and volunteering filled this need and provided a great mood boost. Keeping a gratitude journal at the end of the day is highly beneficial when trying to focus on what you do have versus what you don't have. Sometimes it is good to just sit back and count your blessings.

Anisha feels she is still in a state of limbo while she awaits her Social Security disposition. I recommended that she come up with an alternative plan in case she is denied again. She may have to come up with her own business or check out work-from-home options. It beats starving.

"We must accept finite disappointment, but never lose infinite hope."
–Martin Luther King, Jr.

CORDELL

I'm here because I started having thoughts of harming myself. I am not where I want to be in life. At 25, I was in a car accident. The other driver was drunk. I am paralyzed from the waist down and am wheelchair-bound. Now, in my forties, I am forced to reside with my parents after being in and out of the hospital for the past year as a result of several infections. Prior to this, I was independent, working and living on my own.

I guess my parents have good intentions, but they treat me like a child, but it is like my parents are opposed to the idea of me living independently. They have something to say about everything I do. Whether I go out with friends, or friends come over, or if I leave a light on, there's always something to complain about. They got something to say about the way I spend my own money. Man, I just started thinking things would be better off if I was no longer around. Over and over, I considered overdosing on pills. I saw visions of me killing myself, but ultimately I changed my mind. I called a friend who called 911.

Plus, I have never really dealt with being paralyzed in the prime of my life . . . I think I'm ready now.

The Mess

Cordell suffers from depression and self-doubt because of his injury. Though it happened years ago, he remains deeply affected by the accident, and he has not dealt with his paralysis.

Cordell's Mindset

Cordell is afraid of causing conflict and so refuses to express to his parents or anyone how he really feels. He is a people-pleaser. Deep down inside, there is a lot of anger because he is paralyzed, but he does not express it.

Miracle Question Response

You know, living on my own again would make me happy. Getting back to work would make me happy. I would have peace.

Solution

Cordell is a peaceful person who needed to break free of his mother. He wanted to do many things, but she would tell him he could not, and self-doubt would settle in. After starting the process to locate handicapped housing, he regained some of his zest for life, looked forward to returning to work, and became one of the most motivated clients I have ever worked with. He was ready to deal with being paralyzed, ready to let go of his anger, and ready to move forward. However, I think deep inside he was angry, and this anger needed to be expressed.

"He who has health, has hope; and he who has hope, has everything."
—Thomas Carlyle

ADDICTION

No one wants to be an addict. No one comes out of the womb and says, "I want to be an alcoholic or an addict when I grow up." Many addicts I have worked with have had some horrible experiences during their lifetimes and developed unhealthy and addictive habits to cope and survive. By the time you are an addict, you no longer derive any pleasure from using; you use only to avoid the pain of withdrawing. The goal is to find new ways to deal with the pain and manage your issues. I never lecture anyone who is dealing with addiction. An addict told me years ago, "When you are ready to quit, you will quit. Those programs are for those who still need convincing that they need to quit." I have seen too many family members and concerned love ones adamantly affirm that someone needs this program or this program. You can put an addict in the best program in the universe; if he or she has not hit rock bottom and made the decision to quit, it will most likely result in relapse.

Understand that relapse is often a part of recovery. I worked with a gentleman who had 30 years of recovery and lost it by walking by the alcohol section at a Wal-Mart. Currently, most treatment programs paint everyone with the same brush stroke, and I think this is a disservice to clients.

TAMARA

Being in therapy has been a part of my life for so long that I don't remember a time without it. I recently moved back to my hometown; being closer to my family seemed like a good idea. I thought I was getting better, but I am actually getting worse. I just got out of the hospital. I had been admitted because of my depression, my schizophrenia, anxiety, alcohol abuse, and crack cocaine use. It's the depression that really gets to me. I managed to stay sober for a year once, when I was pregnant with my son. My use got out of control when I was 20, after my mom died. I just couldn't take the pain of losing her. She was my rock. I've been relying on them for so long that my body is starting to give up on me in my thirties, and I just can't cope. I sleep all day, have no appetite, and I am so thin. It scares me to look in the mirror. I always try to be good about taking my meds, but because of insurance issues, when I moved back home, I had to go without them.

Crack has become my coping mechanism when my husband yells at me. I did not grow up in a household where there was yelling and screaming. He did. Our relationship has never been that great. He comes from a dysfunctional family. They all drink and use drugs. My family is close-knit and very supportive, even though I'm a wreck. Because we are so different, his family often tells me that I think I am better than them, and so does he.

We haven't made love in five years, and that's fine by me. I really do not have an interest in sex with him. He does not allow me to go out to work, saying my job is to stay at home and take care of him and our kids. I don't have a problem with the concept of women being homemakers. My husband is so controlling, he holds the purse strings, so he holds the power. This makes me feel so helpless.

I am so depressed. All day, I just sit in the dark and sleep my life away. This seems to help. Shutting the world out seems to help. I only leave the house if I really have to. I love my children so much, but I am in such a crap state that I am really battling to take care of them. I know I need help. I have to find the strength to get it, to ask for it, but I'm scared. I just have to keep on telling myself that it's the best thing, that it's what I have to do, for my children, if for no one else. We split up for a year, and it was very nice and peaceful.

I am the black sheep of my family. My brothers and sisters are all college graduates, have successful careers and happy lives. My mom was my rock though, she was always there for me, always looked out for me. When she died, my brothers told me that "momma ain't around to help you now." As mean as this sounds, my family helps me when I'm really in need. They are disappointed in me. I was smart in school. I got good grades in school, and I was expected to succeed. I don't know how I wound up like this. At times, I do think of suicide, but I can't do it because of my children.

The Mess

Tamara had inadequate coping skills, lost her identity, and has low self-esteem because she feels inferior to her siblings. She has suicidal ideations with thoughts of leaving here.

Tamara's Mindset

She believes she was not good enough and feels she does not measure up to her siblings.

Miracle Question Response

I would not be on drugs. Life would be fun again.

Solution

Tamara is self-sacrificing and kind hearted. Tamara needed to identify what she wanted her life to look like and stop being afraid to dream of a better one. Whenever she tried to envision a brighter future, she would beat herself up about her shortcomings. She would think of a goal and talk herself out of it, telling herself she wasn't capable of making it happen, thus spiraling back into depression. I recommended she stop focusing so much on her husband and focus more on identifying what she needed to be healthy emotionally, physically, and psychologically. I suggested that the next time he started yelling, instead of cowering, she could seek space away from him. If necessary, leave and calmly say "I'll be back when you stop yelling." Again, I do not give advice as to whether one should terminate a relationship. That is a personal decision. When a relationship is bad and you have had enough, no one will have to tell you to leave. I do not know whether Tamara ever took these suggestions to heart. She missed the subsequent sessions. I attempted to call her, but the number was disconnected.

"Sometimes you need to get out of your own way." –Author unknown

BRANDON

I'm interested in counseling because I need help with what looks like the end of my 25-year marriage. You see, I'm an alcoholic, and my wife has had enough of my drinking, and she wants out. She wants a divorce, but I want to try to make things work. I want to be there for my boys, and I love my house, my home. She says she can't take it anymore. It's not like I'm a mean drunk. I drink and stay to myself to cope.

I drink because of her. She's a nagging witch. The more she nagged, the more I drank. On average, I would drink anything from three to four beers on a weekday and between eight and ten on weekends. I drink to feel good. I had forgotten how to feel good without the booze. I'm scared of having to leave. Scared of losing my four sons. I'm going to miss the family vacations, raising my boys, doing the yard work, working on projects around the house.

Mostly I'm scared of what it is going to do to me financially. My lawyer warned me that I will take a hit. Really, I planned to retire in a couple of years. I don't believe that would be possible now. My wife didn't work, because she had spent our marriage at home taking care of me and the kids.

When the court ordered me to leave my home, it hurt to the core of my heart. I moved in with my brother and sister-in-law. It's not so bad. They were so happy to see me leave my wife anyway. They too saw her as a witch from hell and really did not care for her much. My brother and his wife are rarely home, and their house needs a lot of work, which was great for me. Working on their house gives me something to do. I need to have a purpose, and this made me feel needed and useful.

The Mess

Brandon was not happy. He was depressed with his wife and depressed with the thought of living without his family. Coping by drinking distracted him from his marital problems but did not solve any of his problems.

Brandon's Mindset

You must be dutiful. You stay with your wife and take care of your family, even if it costs you your own peace.

Miracle Question Response

I would not have the urge to drink. My wife and I would work out our problems.

Solution

Brandon is gentle in nature. He is dutiful. However, Brandon neglected to mention he had a DUI charge, and this is what really prompted him to seek counseling. He needed several letters stating that he was involved in counseling to present to the court before sentencing. It is simply considerate that you reveal to your therapist beforehand if you need any forms or letters completed for attorneys, court, Social Security, or FMLA. This paperwork can be very time consuming, and it is very frustrating when clients hide this information.

Brandon had good family support, and he soon understood why he had to leave his wife. Brandon needed to set boundaries in regards to what he was willing to tolerate from his wife. As he began to improve, she often attempted to draw him back into their drama by starting arguments, but instead of being caught up, he would leave. He stopped the dance with her where she would push his buttons, and he would resort to drinking. This threw her off. He stopped drinking and refused to fall prey to her attempts to engage him in arguments on his visits. She needed help with the house, so he still does things around the house, not solely for her, but for his sons.

Ultimately, leaving his wife and family was not as bad as he thought it would be. He was happier, still had regular contact with his boys – whom he adores – and his sons were very understanding. Brandon no longer had the urge to drink. He found a peace and happiness he had not had in quite some time. The projects at his old house and at his brother's kept him busy, and they were very appreciative of his help. He also started golfing again – another thing that brought him happiness.

When you are ready to quit, you'll quit. Those programs are for those who still need convincing. –Author unknown

RELATIONSHIPS

As humans, we have a need to relate to others. At least, most of us do. Our drives and motivations in life develop and operate within the context of our early relationships, particularly the primary relationship with our initial caregivers. Our early relationships, consciously and unconsciously, influence our later relations with others.

Imagine an infant who is not cuddled and caressed and whose mother or caregiver is in and out or gone for long periods of time. Do you think this individual develops confidence and trust and believes his or her needs will be met? Does this infant have the ability to trust later in life? All of this plays out in our later relationships.

Two books I strongly recommend for women struggling with relationship issues are Kara King's *The Power of the Pussy* and Steve Harvey's *Act Like a Lady, Think Like a Man*. In my opinion, both books show that women have really given up their power. I love both of these books because they point out that women are of value and possess certain qualities and can make things happen just by the nature of being a woman. Both books explain that a man of substance wants a woman of substance and confidence.

I look to the lower animal kingdom a lot in an attempt to understand human behavior and to remove the emotional biases and personal constructs that often occur when doing so. In most animal species, the male is the pursuer, or chases the female. Personally, I do not believe women should chase or beg a man for anything; it's against nature. The egg does not chase the sperm. The male peacock ruffles his feathers in an effort to attract the female. The male rat builds a nest to attract the female.

If the male rat does not build a nest for her, she finds another rat. The female rat does not beg and plead with the male rat, nor does she try to turn him into what she wants him to be. She simply goes and finds another rat who will build a nest for her. Do rats have more sense than we do?

Rarely do I go out but when I do, I observe women in bars and clubs; they look so lonely and desperate. Bust-outs, or undesirable men, pick up on this and hone in on these women. The women they target often know deep in their hearts that these men are not suitable for them or are up to no good, but out of desperation and loneliness or for whatever reason, they try to change them into what they need them to be which, if it works, usually only works temporarily because they are going to be who they are eventually.

One of my male cousins told me early on to set your standards so high that if you come down a little you are still superior. Women set low standards then complain when a man rises up and meets those low standards. Set the bar high, and a man of substance will rise up; the bust-outs will hem and haw and say you are high maintenance and want too much. Draw a flowchart of the men or women you have dated. Describe characteristics of each person. You should see a pattern and will discover it is you who keeps selecting a certain type of man. Your selections are a reflection of you.

Another big mistake I see women make is complaining about their previous partners to their new mates. Say, for instance, your previous partner did 30 things for you. If your new partner comes along and does 31 things for you, he thinks he is "Captain Save-A-Hoe." How do you think a man would respond if you said to him, without bragging, that your previous partner was a good person who loved you and was very supportive and cooked and cleaned and was a good provider? Now, a bust-out would respond "why the hell you ain't with him?" but a man of substance would know exactly what he had to do to be with you. He has a choice to rise up or keep it moving.

Additionally, women make the mistake of putting all their hopes and dreams into one man and relentlessly attempting to force him into her dreams. This really isn't fair to the man, who may or may not have the capacity to be what she needs him to be. Sometimes on the first date, women have walked a man down the aisle and planned their entire future together instead of letting the relationship evolve on its own. When a woman gives her heart and soul, and it is usually to the wrong man, she is usually giving the man what she so desperately wants to receive in return. When it is not reciprocated, look out. Here comes, "Look at what all I gave you and all I have done for you, and you can't do this, that, or the other for me." She becomes bitter, angry, and sometimes violent. Love comes with conditions.

Men, on the other hand, tend to associate themselves with several women. When one is deemed suitable, that's who he decides to settle down with. This is the one he will do just about anything for and will capture his heart. I am not suggesting that women sleep around with several men. I am suggesting that women enjoy the company of several men, then decide who is worthy of her.

SHANTE

Why do I keep picking the wrong men instead of learning from my past mistakes? I am depressed, can't sleep, sad, and tired.

I just can't be with Andre. He is emotionally unavailable and cold towards me. I'm just disgusted. Why do I end up with the wrong man instead of learning from my past? There is no way in hell I want to reach my forties still feeling the same way.

I wanted to be married badly. I know I sounded like a broken record, repeatedly asking him, "Why can't you 'wife' me?" Part of the problem was that he is obviously still involved with his other children's mother. We have argued many times about her. I played the, "I'm the better bitch" game with her. She would do something for him, and I would do something better to top what she did. She don't have her shit together like me. I do way more for him, so why would any man want to walk away from all I have to offer?

More than anything I wanted a stable, two-parent household and the family, something I didn't have growing up. I cannot understand why he would not want all I'm trying to offer him and would rather deal with her.

I know marriage was not on Andre's radar until he lost his apartment. All of a suddenly, he was interested in marriage, and he "wifed" me. With four, plus one on the way, I thought life would be different. Instead, he became very strict and punitive with my children. Yet I still played the role of housewife "to the T" and I was proud to be a wife. I was so glad to check off "married" on my son's birth certificate when he was born.

I saw the glaring red flags but ignored them. I know my husband is still involved with his children's mother, and he even brought her into our home without my permission or knowledge, until his oldest daughter told me. I believe he was attempting to show his children's mother how good he was living.

I hooked up with a carbon copy of my first two children's father. He too was emotionally cold towards me and used and abused my kindness. Day one, I questioned Andre's fidelity, yet I tenaciously tried to build a life with him and was loyal to him. I liked him because he seemed different from the other guys I dated. He spent time with my son and played with him and helped him with his homework.

Now my struggle is to get out of this marriage. I know I still talk about him non-stop, but I love him. I don't know why, but I love him. At the same time, I'm angry at him. You know, I believe something happened between him and my oldest daughter. He became real mean to her.

The Mess

Shante's depression stemmed from being desperate for someone to love her and not getting what she wanted in childhood. She still carries the scars of her difficult childhood, where she was left on her own at a young age and became a rebellious teenager. She does not learn from her mistakes and keeps repeating them and keeps looking for men to give her what she did not get from her father.

Shante's Mindset

Shante believes that what she gives will be returned and that, with a man, she will overcome her childhood issues. She just wants to be loved.

Miracle Question Response

I would have my shit together. I was doing so well. I was in school; my kids were independent. I just need to get back on track.

Solution

Shante has the resilience to bounce back after adversity, a hopeful disposition, and some supportive family members. She is just a kind person. She does not seem to learn the lesson from her poor choices, so life sends a more painful experience, and she has yet to learn her lesson. I have been seeing Shante off and on for several years. Shante will probably be a lifelong client. It does not matter if she stops coming to therapy for a couple of months, or even a couple of years; when she is frustrated and has dug a deep enough hole and needs good, sound advice, she will hunt me down, and I can usually get her back on track. She is a beautiful, kind-hearted person who is always quick to help others but just keeps looking for the love she did not get as a child from the wrong men. When you don't learn the lesson, situations are repeated until the outcome is so painful that you end up acknowledging that "I got it, and I won't do that anymore."

For some reason, Shante loved hanging out with people, including family members, who really weren't trying to move forward in the same way that she was. I suggested to her many times that she may need to expand her circle of friends to accomplish the goals she was trying to accomplish.

Everyone should have a sound board of directors that they go to for support and advice. Be careful who you select. For the most part, people don't want to see you advance, and it's best to leave them behind. Don't look for support from them, even when they are your family. In these situations, leaving them behind is exactly what is necessary to keep moving forward. As my aunt used to say, "Give them the light touch, and feed them with a long-handled spoon." Shante needed someone who could give her sound advice in life management and tell her what she needed to hear, as opposed to what she wanted to hear.

Shante got a divorce and became more optimistic but is still focused on her children's father. She is not sure which direction to take. She was all over the place. Whatever Shante pursued, she was bound to do well if she focused, so I suggested that she concentrate on doing one thing at a time and doing it very well, and the universe will open up other opportunities. If she could not manage what she had, it was very unlikely she could manage more if it was given to her.

I explained that she could love her children's father but it didn't mean she had to be with him, because he was clearly not good for her. When he was going through a difficult time, she thought he needed a hug. When she hugged him, she said he was cold and stiff and she realized he may have needed a hug but did not want it from her. She has not been burned enough by her children's father, so she still keeps trying to have some type of relationship with him, and he lets her down each and every time. Shante needs to learn that guys tend to categorize women and this is reflected in the way they will interact with different women. There are women they will consider fit for marriage and women who they deem time-fillers. There are women they will use for money and a place to stay, for sex, and women they will use to their advantage. Know where you stand, and only believe what they show you, not what they say.

She has reached a point where she does not want a man and jokingly said, "I don't even want a man to say hi to me right now." I agree with her that it's time for men to take a back seat so she can get herself together and stay focused on her goals. The test was for her to ask herself if what she was doing, or who she was dealing with, was helping her move toward her goals or away from them. It was important for her to surround herself with people who were moving forward, as she was trying to do, and stop trying to rescue others before she rescues herself. I advised her to always apply the lessons she had learned instead of repeating her mistakes and suggested that she learn to accept people for who they are, not who she needs them to be.

I also suggested that she find someone to look after her children for at least a couple of hours a week so she could have time to herself. I had her write her obituary so that she would become aware that she is not going to live forever. Every second wasted on him could have been time spent on moving forward.

"When someone loves you, they don't have to say it. You can tell by the way they treat you." –Author unknown

BRENDA

I'm in my mid-fifties, and the life I always dreamed of having was not the one I was living. I gave my heart and soul to a guy that left me for another woman four years ago. We lived together for five years until I found out he was seeing a woman from his job. I gave him an ultimatum. It was her or me. I figured, we had five years invested, he would pick me. He chose her. Yeah, I saw the signs. He had become distant and cold towards me. It was as if he hated my touch. He became withdrawn. It had been months since we had sex. Yeah, I knew something was up, but I was willing to do anything to save our relationship. How could he just walk away from me, from us, like I meant nothing to him? You would think after all I gave him, after all I did for him, he would at least value what we had. I still don't believe it.

Yes, four years later I'm still very hurt. My entire world was torn apart. He completely ripped my heart out and has never apologized to me. I thought we could at least be friends. He does not even want to be friends. He ignores my telephone calls, any text messages I send him, and has unfriended me on Facebook. When he gathered his belongings as he left, which really weren't many, I suggested we remain friends. I really don't want to sleep with anyone else and asked him if we could still have sex every once in a while. I thought his relationship with that devil was a passing fling that would fade away. I know one day he is going to come to his senses and realize what he had with me was special. When he refused to just have sex with me, I was hurt even more. I couldn't understand why or how he could do this to me, to us. We really had something special, so I thought. I wanted to marry him so badly, but he swore he would never marry again. But I thought after time, he would change his mind. He married her a year after our breakup.

The months that followed after our split left me scared and alone. I cried. I couldn't eat, I couldn't sleep, and I was a total wreck. Day and night I'd think of him. My visions of him with her drove me insane. One night I hoped I would hear a knock on my door and it would be him. I had been so convinced that our relationship was going to last forever.

My family and friends just told me that it was his loss and their relationship wouldn't last. Well it did, and he married her. None of this consoled me. I still want him. If it were not for her, we would still be together. I'm supposed to be Mrs. Michael M. Anderson, not that devil woman. I really hate that bitch. Her pretty features will eventually fade away. Men always seem to think the grass is greener on the other side. If they would water their own grass, it would be just as green.

I wonder what it is about her that he loves so much. What does she have that I don't have? Why wasn't I good enough for him? I did everything around our home, the cooking, the cleaning, paid all the bills. I was at his total beck and call! I never questioned him when he went out. I respected his space and his privacy. I was a good woman to him!

I pray for the demise of their relationship, even though they are married. He refused to marry me, but he married her! That's okay. I haven't given up. I keep hoping that one day he will come to his senses and realize just how good he had it with me and come running back. When he does, I will be waiting with open arms. I still keep in touch with his family, and they love me. I still send messages to him on Facebook, and I regularly send him text messages. I want to show him that I still love him, even though he ignores me, that I still care for him and that I forgive him. I just want him to come back to me!

The Mess

Brenda has turned one event into prolonged suffering and agony and depression. She tries to display a tough exterior but really has low self-esteem and self-worth, is insecure, hopeless, fearful, scared, and delusional. She is not living in reality and refuses to move on with her life. Therefore, she remains stuck in a prison she built herself.

Brenda's Mindset

"I gave him nine years of my life. The last five, 24/7." The ex should be with her, even though he clearly does not want to be with her and has moved on with his life.

Miracle Question Response

He would leave his wife and show up on my doorstep one night, apologize, say he made a big mistake, and plead for me to take him back.

Solution

She has a very supportive family and friends. Brenda has a kind and giving heart. First, I suggested to Brenda that she take off her rose-colored glasses and understand that this man did not love her the way she wanted him to love her. The signs had been there for quite some time. When I had her write down what she liked and did not like about her ex, the latter list was longer.

He was not affectionate toward her, and she did more for him than he did for her. They also argued a lot. I suggested some reality acceptance was in order because of the fact that he has moved on with his life, gotten married, and was not coming back to her. It really does not matter why he left. The fact is, he is gone, and it is his choice to be with someone else. If she insisted on reminiscing about the relationship and what used to be and what it could have been, she was to analyze the relationship from a stance of reality. She was to identify the lesson she learned so she does not repeat the same mistakes in her next relationship.

Next was to let go, simply because the burden of holding on is heavy. Brenda simply needed to let go, learn the lesson, and move on with her life. Logically, I attempted to get her to process why she would want to hold on to someone who clearly did not want to be with her. If she felt she was wrong or stupid for putting so much hope in someone else, she was to forgive him and herself and move forward.

In my family, the women are taught that you do not cry or trip over anything that is not crying or tripping over you. It's just that simple. I find it odd when women give up their power over a man. Kara King's book *The Power of the Pussy* speaks frankly on the power that women possess. It gives some pretty good suggestions on how women should govern themselves in relationships. My clients love the book.

Brenda turned a one-time painful event into four years and counting of suffering and agony. This time and energy could have been better spent moving on and healing and fully living the life God gave her. I suggested that she delete, suspend, or at least unfriend his friends and family on Facebook and stop sending direct and indirect messages to him.

Saying he is "not shit" and the other derogatory posts said more about her than him. If he was "not shit," then why did she pick him? Why did she stay with him for five years? And why is she still talking about him? Basically, she is broadcasting that a guy ran game on her, and she is mad she got slicked. It is sad to see women do this.

It also sends a signal to the vultures that they can now attempt to hone in on her. Vultures are always circling, waiting for the opportunity to move on in. Her "real talk" and "Amen corner" friends are most likely waiting for her next soap opera post. Everyone should not know your business. Personal business should be known to a select few. I also advised her to stop hanging out where her ex hangs out in an attempt to run into him. Continuing to do so only stymies, or blocks, healing.

The goal is to move toward healing and get into a mindset where she can say, "Thank you for the lesson. God love you, because I tried." She was to work on forgiveness, since she thinks she is owed an apology and feels she was wronged. You have heard it time and time again, forgiveness is really for you, not the other person. The cost of not forgiving is too great. Brenda remains depressed, stuck and pathological.

"The one that broke you cannot be the one to fix you." –Author unknown

MARI

It all started when I got a text message of a picture of my husband cuddled up with another woman. We had been married for twenty years, and this was his third affair. What was different about this one was that it was with my sister. So of course, the gossip circulated amongst family and friends, and everyone knew about it. This time, he had taken humiliating me to a completely new level.

Overwhelmed, I sought counseling for the first time in my life. This time there would be no reconciliation. I want out and filed for a divorce. My greatest fear is losing my home. I love my home. I have decorated every inch of it. It is mine. It is where I raised our sons.

Sometimes I'm glad he is gone, then wonder if I should take him back. I don't know if the excessive weight I've picked up over the years turned him off, because the other woman is a little bitty thing. I used to be small like that. I questioned if I kept myself attractive enough for him. Did I not work hard enough? It was me who made everything possible and kept everything together, from our family, to our beautiful home, to the lavish family vacations.

The thought of facing family and friends overwhelmed me with anxiety, and I started to have panic attacks. I just knew that someone would ask me questions about the affair. To my surprise, my ex-husband did not contest the divorce and did not want anything from me. We are now divorced, and I'm relieved. I'm faced with starting my life over and don't know where to start. This is scary. I don't even know where to start. Date? I haven't been on a date in 25 years. What do you do on a date? I'm free. Free to do what?

The Mess

She was depressed because she now had to reinvent her life. What she thought would be is no more. Frequently, she had trouble making decisions and would overthink things, always expecting the worse. She had become reclusive to her home and avoided family. The children were grown, and now she had a lot of free time that she did not know what to do with it.

Mari's Mindset

Everything was just hopeless. She was open to finding a new love but felt the pickings were slim. She was lonely.

Miracle Question Response

I would be in a relationship. I got through the divorce. A companion, someone to do things with and enjoy life.

Solution

To focus on the good things in her life, she has a very supportive and close knit family, four beautiful sons, and five grandchildren. She started to get out more, but she still feels a void. Admittedly, she wanted to be in a relationship. Her spirits really dipped when her ex-husband married the woman he had an affair with. Mari quit her job and wound up getting another job. She travels quite a bit with some friends but is still struggling to find direction for her life. She has not recaptured her happiness.

I advised Mari to focus on the progress she had made through, and immediately after, her divorce. She was also to stop avoiding family activities and spend more time with family and friends. Mari attempted to date but found it depressing because the men she went out with had so many problems. She loved to travel and do things, and guys were always missing-in-action in these areas. When she started trying to justify one guy's shortcomings, I stopped her and advised her not to compromise.

Too often, women lower their standards, and when the guy meets the low standards, women get mad and complain about the guy. Raise your standards. A guy who truly cares for you will rise up to them. By no means does this mean being unrealistic. Have some idea of what you want in a guy, and know what you are willing to compromise on and what you refuse to compromise.

It was imperative that she continue to work on herself and start identifying what she wants in a man and setting some standards. She had to start trusting her gut and stop ignoring red flags that were bright, red, and flapping in the wind right in her face. Instead of trying to fix a broken man, she needed to reinvent her own life and realize that the right man was out there somewhere, no assembly required. She still struggles with desiring a mate but is dealing with it.

"Just because the past didn't turn out like you wanted it to, doesn't mean your future can't be better than you've ever imagined."
–Author unknown

DUANE

I was born and raised in the streets. My family sold drugs, dominated the block, and controlled the neighborhood turf. I was never pressured to adopt the street life. I made that decision on my own, but when I did make that choice to join the family business, they made sure I was equipped with all the necessary tools to get the job done and done right! Reputation is everything in the streets, and it was made clear to me from the jump that I had to uphold it. I've been on both ends of a gun and, from time to time, I still get flashbacks of those days I spent running the streets. I've got several numbers, and I've been in the joint several times. They say I'm bipolar, but I ain't bipolar, and I'm not going to take those pills that they give you for it. I tried taking those pills but didn't like the way they made me feel. I'm here because of anger issues, and I'm trying to stay in school. I want to be an attorney.

I'm trying to leave the street life behind, but these young cats keep trying me. The old heads know me, and I still get my respect from all the

OGs. But I've had enough of that world. I don't go out much now, except to family events, and I keep to myself. All I want do is stay on the right path and live a peaceful life. I want to set my conscience free because, believe me, the things you witness on the streets can definitely mess with your mind and make it hard to keep balanced. What am I to do when these young cats want to push up on me? I'm not a punk, and I'm not gone' back down. I'm capable of snatching the life outta one of them just like that!

Then there is my girl. I swear I love her, but when she gets all up in my face, yelling, screaming, cursing and kicking up a fuss, I just can't stand it. She's got her own issues, but I'll never hit a woman. In spite of all of her crazies, I care about her. I love her. But sometimes she just keeps going at me. It takes all I have not to snap. Me and my girl, we split up, and I moved in with my brother. Here I am in my forties, and I sleep in my brother's basement. That ain't cool at all.

My girl and I are cool. We get along, seeing as we've got a daughter together. I ain't even thinking about replacing her with another woman, but I am a man with manly needs. As things stand now, I don't even have no interest in other women. I thought the breakup would send me into some crazed frenzy, but it didn't. During our break up, I never got intimately involved with any other woman. Although she'd try to push my buttons and get me heated by starting unnecessary arguments, I don't engage. She calls during all times of the night. I knew that was her way of keeping tabs on me, just to see if I was home or with someone, or out in the streets. That ain't me no more.

Duane's Mindset

He still has a street mindset. "You have to maintain your reputation and show no fear. You don't let anyone punk you. You have to handle every battle."

Miracle Question Response

I would not be so angry. I would marry my girlfriend, and we would live happily ever after. I would have my own cleaning business and go to law school.

Solution

Duane is a family-oriented guy. He comes from a very close, protective family. If you cross one, you have crossed them all, and you best always be on the look-out. I got him to develop some short-term and long-term goals to focus on. I needed him to understand that the "cats" in the streets did not have anything to lose – he did. He had a girlfriend he loved and a family. I asked if going back to jail over these "zero minuses" in the street was worth it. He was to think of this when he felt himself going from to zero to fifty and leave the situation immediately. With his girlfriend, I suggested he use the broken record technique. Just keep presenting his stance that he loved her and wanted to be with her and will do anything for her. I advised him to avoid escalating arguments, even if someone pushes his buttons. All of this has worked well for him.

He has started his cleaning business and is working on getting his own place. Duane said, "I always hear what you tell me in the back of my head." He goes to the gym on a regular basis, and this has been a good outlet for him to release pent-up anger and frustration.

His girlfriend wants to reunite. Since he is separated from his girlfriend, he is in a good position to set some boundaries with her and maintain them. I advised him to set some boundaries, and make them known to her, regarding what he would and would not tolerate and to know that he would not be anyone's puppet. It was decided that if they got back together, there would be no more putting anyone out. You put people out when you are in danger, or if the relationship has ended for real, not just because you are mad at the moment. Now was a good time to suggest that she get some help from a professional because he said she had issues of her own to work through.

For the most part, Duane is content and pretty much stays at home and watches TV. He adds that he is getting comfortable with himself and is okay being by himself. Most of all, he does not anger so easily.

"Once you learn how to be happy, you won't tolerate being around people who make you feel anything less." –Author unknown

SEXUAL ASSAULT

There is no doubt that suffering through sexual assault and abuses as a child or an adult is one of the most horrific ordeals anyone can experience, male or female. It violates a person in such an indescribable way. Often, the perpetrator is someone known to the victim. The number-one perpetrator of child sexual assault is a mother's boyfriend or stepfather, followed by other relatives and close family friends. I have only worked with a handful of individuals who were attacked or abused by a total stranger. The horrible experience is not limited to the time it occurred; it remains a traumatic event for the rest of one's life. I work with a 78-year-old woman who describes her two childhood rape ordeals like they happened yesterday.

Victims usually hide a lifetime of pain before they decide to talk about the abuse. They often stay silent because the trauma left them paralyzed and fearful or simply in disbelief. No matter how much we say, "Tell someone," many people do not until adulthood. While traumatic and paralyzing, one can learn to live again and not let these kinds of tragic experiences remain a part of, or define, their entire life.

Some of the stories above were traumatic stories of sexual abuse over which the individuals had no control. Each woman has chosen to pursue a better life through the aid of therapy. There is no one way to deal with trauma. Non-traditional therapy, such as yoga, expressive art, and pet therapy, is showing promising results with victims of trauma, and helping others who had a similar experience was very helpful for Zuri. But there is no quick and easy answer to get a grip on trauma. It takes time –

probably a lifetime – to make the incident a part of your life and not your entire life.

I also suggest some form of aggressive exercise like one of my patients, Viola, does. She decided to take up tennis. Kickboxing, racquetball, running, and power walking are other sports that may allow for a healthy physical release of emotions. Beside the cardiovascular and physical benefits, exercise has been proven to alleviate depression, anxiety, and stress symptoms. It increases the neurotransmitter norepinephrine, which aids in the stress response. Physical activity can take your mind off your troubles, even if only temporarily, and exercising can be calming, thereby reducing anxiety. Physical activity releases endorphins, the happy hormones responsible for the euphoric feeling after exercise and improved mood; serotonin, which regulates mood, appetite, and sleep; and dopamine, and the ability to experience pleasure and pain is also affected by exercise.

These are the same hormones that anti-depressants and anti-anxiety medications affect. Why not get them naturally without the risk of side effects? The results are instant. Antidepressants and anti-anxiety medications take four to six weeks to become therapeutic. If you don't want to resort to medication but claim you don't have time for exercise, then I guess you will remain depressed. If it is important to you, you will find a way.

Personally, I believe that the PTSD associated with sexual abuse should be tackled with a multi-faceted approach, because there is no one set way of dealing with it. It is about finding what works for you.

VIOLA

In my mid-seventies, I consider myself in great shape for my age. I'm not one of those fragile, helpless old women. I am a firm, direct and to the point kind of woman, and anyone who doesn't like it is welcome to get lost. You can't work for the post office all your life and be a pushover. I recently retired, not because I was tired and ready to stop working; I did it to get my family off my back. I don't know what their problem is, really.

They keep telling me that I'm mean, but I don't see how standing your ground makes you mean. When I am right, I am right, and I will always admit when I am wrong. So what the problem is, I just do not know.

I guess the truth is that I don't like being this way. I know I'm hardened because of my past. My childhood was really rough, and I had to get tough to survive. My mother and I lived in a small bedroom of a boarding house in Atlanta. There was only one bed, and my mother slept in that while I slept on a mattress on the floor. Our life was cool until my mother hooked up with a man who introduced her to the taste of alcohol. He would stay over a couple of nights a week, and they would have sex while I was on the floor. They didn't care that I was there, that I could hear them. It was awful.

The weekends were the worst. Every weekend there was a party. Parties attended by the neighborhood locals looking to let their hair down after a hard week. I was only twelve years old when one of the frequent patrons decided to get his thrill by feeling on my already well-developed butt. When I told my mother, she told me that Mr. Wilson was a good man and wouldn't do anything like that to a little girl. I couldn't believe it and still can't believe how my mother could not believe me and just dismissed my cry for help, just like that. I felt so vulnerable and unprotected.

I had to get away from it, so I would spend nights with a friend who lived over the road. This was a great arrangement until I woke up one night to find a man on top of me. My friend was lying beside me in the same bed. The intruder had a gun with him and told us that he would kill us if we screamed. He then brutally raped me.

They took me to the hospital, but this was before the time of rape kits, and there was no such thing as rape counseling. They reported the attack in the local newspaper, and the people in the neighborhood looked for the guy, but no one could find him. They all knew it was me though. They all knew that I was the girl who got raped. The other kids were so cruel about it. They teased and ridiculed me, shamed me and made me feel like such crap! I can still hear their voices saying, "Was it good to you, Viola? Did he have a big dick? Did you enjoy it?" Kids can be so cruel and mean.

Then everything went from bad to worse; my mother became an alcoholic, lost her job, and we became homeless. Sometimes we were lucky enough to find somewhere where we could sleep together, other times we had to sleep in different places. Some of the other women in the neighborhood tried to help my mother, but the alcohol had taken over.

To this day I don't know why, but when I was thirteen I started having sex with guys, all different ones. By the time I was fifteen I was pregnant, pregnant and homeless. I was lucky enough to be taken in by one of the other women in the neighborhood. She was so good to me, gave me shelter, food, guidance and, most of all, some peace.

My mother became even more helpless, and it completely broke my heart to see her lying drunk in the street. I couldn't look at her. I would just walk by and pretend that I hadn't even noticed her. I remember one night, I was called to the hospital because my mother had been admitted. I expected the doctor to tell me how to care for her, only to be told she was nothing but a drunk, and he just walked away.

At first, the father of my baby didn't want to have anything to do with either of us. He totally denied that my baby was his at the urging of his family. All of a sudden, he changed his mind and wanted to marry me. After he had initially denied he was the father of my child, I didn't want to be bothered with him. He joined the military and became quite successful and owned his own gas station. He had already betrayed me so much.

One night, while at a club, I thought I had found my knight in shining armor. There was this fine, really handsome man; he took my breath away. I was convinced that there was no way he would want me with my big old, huge pregnant belly. To my surprise, he did, and he married me, and his family took me in and accepted me and my baby as his own. Finally, my life was getting on track. Finally, I was finding some happiness.

It didn't take long for my Prince Charming to turn into a frog and a nightmare. He became physically and mentally abusive. He would hit me until I was black and blue all over. Eventually I got up the courage to leave him. I had to go on welfare to support my kids and myself. For years, he would often just show up at my door, beat the crap out of me, and have sex with me.

It seemed that my life was destined to be filled with men who beat the crap out of me. My second husband also beat the shit out of me. After leaving a club, a friend and I were walking down the street toward three men. Two of them put a bag over his head, and they abducted me and threw me into the back seat of a car. I begged for my life, telling these men that I had seven children at home. As my attacker proceeded to rape me, he asked why I wasn't at home with my kids but instead in the streets.

It took me until I was in my sixties to finally meet a man who was kind, caring, and a good provider. He actually loved me. Then one night he had a massive heart attack, and I lost the only man I had ever loved, the only man I had ever been able to trust. Then four of my closest friends died too. I lost anyone that cared about me. So much abandonment.

The Mess

The biggest mess in Viola's life was hate—justifiably so—and the refusal to forgive. Viola was full of rage, though she had tried to bury it. But as hard as she tried, she could not contain the rage nor the fear, hate, abandonment, and loss. I believe this was a major contributor to several mini-strokes she suffered. Pressure bursts pipes, and her rage spilled forth, hitting her and those who were closest to her.

It was easy to see why she held on to such destructive anger. In her youth, those who should have protected her—her mother, her family, the system, and the community—did not. When she did become attached to someone who sincerely cared about her—the lady who took her in when she was pregnant, her last husband, and close friends—they died.

I asked Viola to think about who she hated the most. Initially, she said her mother, who was a good mother up until the time she started drinking. However, Viola learned that her mother had been sexually abused by her father and later believed that her mother's first drink was probably the first time her mother felt okay. So, she concluded she did not hate her mother; she hated her behavior.

The person she truly hated the most was the first man to rape her. She said that he destroyed her innocence and the rest of her life, not only physically but mentally. For years, she blamed herself for the attack. It wasn't until she went to therapy for that specific issue that she learned to forgive herself. A pastor explained to her that even if she was walking down the street butt naked, no one had a right to violate her. Viola began to complete exercises intended to teach her forgiveness and acceptance, and they allowed her to logically process the tragic events of her life and realize that none of it was her fault. In spite of this enlightenment, she found that her rage was never fully contained. Whenever she heard of the death or rape of a woman in the news, it triggered her PTSD, and she wrestled with her past again and again.

Viola's Mindset
Viola felt she had to have a calloused exterior, but deep down, she still yearned to be loved and protected. Even though she believed that being nice made her too vulnerable, she desperately wanted to feel again.

But every time she let her guard down, she was hurt; this led to the lifelong cycle of disappointment and anger.

Miracle Question Response

I would not have problems with rage, anger, and abandonment. People would not think I was so mean, and I would be a little softer.

Solution

She has seven beautiful, college-educated children that love her. She was tough as leather and overcame a difficult life. The goal was to find a productive outlet for the rage. All of the people who hurt her are deceased, so it was not possible for her closure to come from confronting them directly. So first, I suggested that she write a letter to every person who had harmed or mistreated her, telling them how she felt, then burn it. Writing her feelings down on paper and burning it symbolized release, and she was to do it as often as she needed.

Then, I suggested she engage in a sport to release the tension. Viola had taken up tennis in the past, and she wanted to either return to it, or try racquetball. Now that she was retired, she had more than enough time. I also suggested she engage in some type of creative expression; this technique has been very successful with cancer patients, war veterans, and other survivors of trauma. Viola always wanted to learn how to draw, and she signed up for a class for free at the local community college. She is now learning to foster a gentler disposition.

"It is not what happens to you, but how you react that matters."
–Epictetus

ZURI

The movie *Precious*, if you are unfamiliar with it, is the adaptation of the life of a real woman who suffered immeasurable abuses at the hands of her parents. The titular character, Precious, is repeatedly raped by her father, resulting in two pregnancies, and her mother does nothing to stop it, instead abusing Precious mentally and physically herself. Though the end is uplifting, the story's beginning is one of horror, and it has nothing on the story of my client, Zuri.

Until I was six, I lived in a crack house with my aunt and her men friends. There were so many people in and out of the house. I remember stepping over bodies to move about the house. There was another couple and about seven other kids who lived in the same house. Since I was so young, I grew up thinking that this was my family. The grown-ups had sex with the kids, including me, and would force me and the other kids to have sex with each other. I did not attend school until I was six. Not only did I not have clothes and shoes, I didn't have a birth certificate because my mother gave birth to me on a bathroom floor. One night the police raided the house when a woman in the neighborhood noticed me and one of the other children begging for food. I was placed under child protection, and I was put in foster care. This is when my hell really began.

My foster mother was mean and strict. I had to ask permission for everything. She kept the refrigerator door locked, and the other foster children and I had to ask her for everything from personal hygiene products; like sanitary napkins, soap, and toothpaste; to essentials, like food. She would often go out and leave me in charge of the other kids, but I couldn't control those kids, and I would get in trouble when they misbehaved.

When I was nine, her son tried to push up on me. To get him off, I threw bleach on him. No one believed that I was just trying to defend myself, so they sent me away. This was the start of being placed in residential institutional facilities. There was one out in the county where the men of the town would wait outside the fence for the girls to sneak out through a hole and have sex with them for money, candy, or just some attention. Then there was the place in the city where one of the girls got high on acid and jumped off the roof right in front of us. One minute we were playing and the next, she was spattered on the ground right in front of us.

I would smoke a lot of pot to numb my emotions and to make the pain go away. One day I was in the shower, and one of the staff members at the institution cornered me in the shower. He raped me anally and blamed it on one of the other kids. I was labeled a troublemaker, and they bounced me around from institution to institution, but every time I got into trouble, I was merely defending myself and ended up the one in trouble. I would tell my caseworkers, but they didn't seem to care. They did nothing about it. I gave up on therapy 'cause I got so sick of having to relive the shit over and over again. I got so sick of talking about it.

Every once in a while, the agencies would parade us around for people looking to adopt kids. I wished so hard to be picked. I wished my mom would come and get me and take me away. One day, my mother did show up. I was hanging out in the courtyard with my friends one afternoon when I was fifteen. A woman walks up and says, "I'm your mother."

She's still on drugs and has all the problems using drugs come with, so I'm not sure if I'm happy having my mother in my life.

When I was young, holidays and birthdays meant nothing to me. You can't miss what you never had. To this day, they mean very little to me, but I celebrate holidays and special occasions only to see my son smile. I know that I am one of the lucky ones. So many of my friends who were in the system with me got hooked on drugs and ended up in abusive relationships.

I find it hard to trust people, and I am very suspicious of people. I hate going outside. I feel safer inside. I only go out when I have to, like when I have to buy groceries or take my son out.

I'm so lucky to have my little son. It's because of him that I decided to try therapy again. My screams from the nightmares are starting to upset my son.

The Mess

Zuri suffers from nightmares, flashbacks, and agoraphobia, and she longs for safety, protection, and a sense of belonging.

Zuri's Mindset

The world is a dangerous place. She numbed herself and suppressed desires, wishes, and emotions to survive emotionally and psychologically. As much as she attempts to suppress the human nature to feel loved, secure, and connected, she strongly desires to belong to, and attach to, people.

Miracle Question Response

I don't desire to change what happened to me. There are people who grew up with their parents and they got problems too. Maybe I had to go through this to learn some lessons that I would not have learned had this not happened to me. Mainly, I want to be able to sleep without having the nightmares and flashbacks.

Solution

In therapy, she decided what she wanted to talk about, since she said she did not want to keep reliving her trauma. When she did talk about her trauma, it was as if she transcended to another point in time. The energy in the room changed to stillness, and there was nothing but dead silence and her voice. Afterwards, she always appeared refreshed. Over the years, Zuri agreed to share her life with several of the classes I taught at the local university, and she is always one of the favorite and most touching guest lecturers. She decided to volunteer to help other girls in a community program who have gone through trauma, and this has been very beneficial. She gets a lot of pleasure hearing their stories and offering advice. She is able to help because she has actually been through what they have been through and her approach is not just based on a theory.

Recovery for her has been just talking about whatever she wanted to and a belief in God. She states this is what has gotten her through early adulthood. "When you believe in God and forgive, it allows you to move forward and have a life." She says it begins with baby steps. "God is key. God is first. Without God, there is nothing." Zuri shared that she has encountered people who have experienced horrible things who don't believe in God. They feel that if God truly existed, he would not allow such horrible things to happen. "To understand what happened to you," she would say in response, "you have to go to God."

Zuri accepts that she has horrible experiences in her childhood. However, she reflects that there are people who have experienced worse things than she has. Now she feels she is doing a lot better than most of her cohorts, who wound up doing drugs or living a life in the streets. She is proud that she is not on drugs since both of her parents were on drugs. Her belief is that many of the children whose parents were, or are, addicted had tried drugs to see what could make their parents neglect them. She continues to pray a lot and does not perceive her life as all doom and gloom. She looks at situations differently because "there is always somebody who is worse off than you."

Zuri also says her son keeps her from going crazy. She still struggles with nightmares and going outside and prefers to remain reclusive in her house. Unfortunately, the nightmares are likely to be with her for a while. However, she is a wonderful mother to her son and is in a healthy, intimate relationship with a stable and supportive guy. It is her goal to give her son the life she did not have. This drives her and keeps her focused. Currently, she is doing better than ever. Her conversations in therapy are now about her future and not her past. She has a stronger voice, and I noticed she is more vigilant.

"I'm not worried about anything from the past. Clearing the inside is what makes dreams come true." –Tina Turner

RENA

I sought counseling because, for once in my life, I want to be happy. I have raised my children, and it is time to find out who I am and do me. I need to learn how to take care of myself. I want to figure out what I want in life. I am divorced. I raised my three children alone after my husband

and I split up. I have spent the majority of my adult life keeping busy with work and family, which took my mind completely off the stuff that I had brushed under the rug. My stepfather, who was my mother's boyfriend at the time, sexually abused me when I was a child. I never told my mother about it, and I forgave my stepfather a long time ago. A couple of months ago, I went to a support group, and this has been very helpful. I don't understand why he did what he did to me.

I have become involved with a man I have known since I was 12. It is so hard to trust him because of my past sexual abuse. When he touches me, I cringe. I don't trust men. I feel so vulnerable with my friend, and I don't like feeling this way. This is weird. I like him, and I want to move closer to him, but then I pull away. At times it is like I have no control, and I must be in control. If you are not in control, then you are vulnerable to anything and I will not be vulnerable.

The Mess

Even though she forgave her stepfather, Rena continues to have trust issues with men. She distracts herself from addressing her own issues very well by being good at taking care of others, a common pattern among women. Now Rena wants to confront her demons from the past and learn to take care of herself, but she feels guilty when she places herself first.

Rena's Mindset

Rena's mindset was to tell herself she was okay when she really wasn't. She did not want to rock anyone's boat, which is why she never told her mother about the abuse from her stepfather. This has been her approach for her entire life. Until now, she did not believe she deserved to be treated well and thus became super independent.

Miracle Question Response

I would be happy and would feel good about myself, specifically, I would do more things for myself. This is all I wear, sweat pants and big shirts. I keep my hair in this ponytail. I have two closets full of nice clothes that I don't even wear. I need to wear those clothes. All this weight has to go. I know I picked up all this weight because I'm inactive. For once in my life, I just want to be happy.

Solution

I had Rena complete the life balance wheel to get more detail as to what happiness means to her. Like most of us, doing more fun and recreational things was integral to her recovery. I suggested that she try new things and experiment with things she had always wanted to do but was unable to do because she was always busy raising her children. Doing new things is what keeps life fresh. If we just go to work or school, pay the bills, and take care of others – things we have to do – life can become mundane and boring and this can contribute to depression and anxiety. I also encouraged her to tell her friend how she felt about him and push past the fear. She agreed, and as it turned out, her friend had admired her for quite some time. Being involved with someone involves a certain degree of vulnerability, and problems arise when we do not have some criteria or yardstick or test to determine who we allow ourselves to be vulnerable with.

The start of a relationship introduced another issue for Rena. Like a lot of single mothers, she has had to learn to let go. As a single parent, she was used to taking charge; there was no one else there getting things done but her. However, she is learning to step back a little and let her new beau take charge. As such, the relationship moved forward slowly, which was hard for her because now she felt ready to speed things up. It is like she is trying to make up for lost time. She admits, "I'm a little thirsty."

Currently, she is taking things one day at a time and states that she is finally starting to feel happy. Recently, she became sexually involved with her friend, "which was lovely!" she repeatedly exclaimed. Rena could not stop smiling as she attempted to describe her experience. It was a special experience, thanks to the sexual abuse classes she attended. In addition, she says she feels very emotional now, which she welcomes because suppressing emotions was something she had done for such a long time. Still, being happy is scary because her comfort zone is being in a struggle.

Giggling, she says she no longer feels like a little girl and shared, "I feel like a real woman." Her parents were so controlling, and this is why she left home and got married so young. Since this time, she has been taking care of others. Now she is learning to take care of herself and enjoying life for herself. It is a strange feeling for her, but she is accepting the fact that she deserves something good.

In the back of her mind she still has the "I must be a good girl" image in her head. This is a script from childhood. With a lot of confidence, she says "I am a grown woman, and it's okay, and I can do what I want." Her children see a difference in her. She feels like she has come out of a box and declared that 2016 is her year, and she is going to make it happen.

Rena is noticing that her relationship with others is changing. She states that she feels like a kid, as she is breaking free from her parents' control, from family routines, and what her parents want her to do. Further, she adds that she has been so serious the majority of her life because she thought she needed to be. She realizes she does not have to try to fix everyone else. Rena feels she missed out on a lot because she was always so serious.

She is also learning that most of your family and friends can tolerate you being happy every now and then, but you being happy on a permanent basis, you will most likely encounter some haters. So be prepared. Most of your family and friends cannot envision, encourage, desire, accept, or transcend the limited visions they have for themselves. Be prepared to be happy and have haters surface. Rena was shocked when her children told her that her siblings are not happy that she is happy. No surprise to me, even for this close-knit, enmeshed family who does everything together.

Now she realizes she does not have to try to fix everyone else. She has been everything to everyone else for so long, and she feels guilty when she does for herself. However, she realizes it is important to enjoy life. She is blessed to have her parents and siblings since so many have passed on. She quit her part-time job and realizes she does not need two or three jobs because she does not need stuff to make her happy. She is happy within and feels good on the inside and cries because she is so happy.

"As I began to love myself, my relationship with everyone else changed."
—Author unknown

CHAPTER SIX - SOMETHING TO THINK ABOUT CHANGING YOUR MENTAL MINDSET

Individuals frequently look for some complex therapy or a pill to resolve their depression and anxiety. In reality, it is not some convoluted theory or a medication that is most effective for beating depression and anxiety; it's the simple stuff. The biggest thing you can do to conquer depression and anxiety is change your mental mindset. Your mental mindset is how you think, feel, and act as you experience life. It's your thoughts, perceptions, and actions which determine whether you live a life of depression and anxiety or one of happiness, peace, and calm. "Where your mind goes, your life will follow," says the Dalai Lama.

Whether consciously or unconsciously, many of us have a mental mindset that is programmed to feed depression and anxiety. Some of the biggest contributors to situational depression and anxiety are distorted thoughts, negative perceptions, overthinking, catastrophizing, black and white thinking, unrealistic expectations, and faulty actions or inactions. Your mental mindset's programming started long before your symptoms of depression and anxiety manifested. It was first influenced by the verbal messages, modeling, and experiences you received from your parents and family, significant caregivers, the community you grew up in, schooling, friends, coworkers, your culture, and society.

Think about some of the messages about life and happiness you may have received and internalized over your lifetime. You probably never paid much attention to the verbal scripts you heard or the scenes that played out in front of you as you grew up. Take an honest and accurate look at what you heard and saw during your childhood, and in general, with regards to life and happiness. They had or have a great influence on yours. What did you learn about life and happiness? Ponder significant experiences that may have contributed to your depression and anxiety, because you did not come out of your mother's womb depressed and anxious. Like everything else, you learned it through messages, modeling, and experiences.

What is your current mental mindset? If you do not know, take a real, honest look at your life. Are you optimistic and true to your morals and values? Do you act like yourself and not someone else? Are you enthused? Do you have a zest for life? Is your life full of happiness and joy? Do you learn from your mistakes? If so, your mindset is obviously one of happiness.

On the other hand, are you anxious, pessimistic, and worried? Do you look at the glass as half empty? Do you have low self-esteem? Do you often feel hopeless, tired, and irritable with no motivation and a fear of success? Without a doubt, your mindset is of depression and anxiety.

EVERYONE HAS THE CAPACITY TO CHANGE THEIR LIFE

Take responsibility for everything in your life. Deciding to stop playing the role of victim and blaming everyone else for your life is a good start. Stop justifying your depression and anxiety with "I was abused," "My parents did or did not do this," or "My husband is an asshole/my wife is a bitch." Life is not picking on you. You are not being singled out for doom and gloom. Unfair, awful, and tragic things happen in life and have happened since the beginning of time. Challenges are a part of life and, yes, some of us have more challenges than others. Life isn't fair, and no one ever guaranteed it would be. We all want a happy ending, but sometimes in life, there is no happy ending. However, most of our hell is self-created; more often than not, we are willing participants in conditions that leave us feeling unhappy and miserable. Painful events are turned into years of suffering and agony. Accept that if you are alive, you will have challenges in your life.

It does wonders when you stop complaining, because it keeps you off the path of complacency, inaction, and stagnation. Do not let your entire life revolve around depression and anxiety. Dream, dare, and do something different. Take steps to improve your mood, and stop complaining about your mood. For a full week, count how many times during the day you complain about your life. While there is no exact number for an acceptable amount of complaining, it will familiarize you with your negative patterns. So the next time you start complaining, stop yourself.

This may be a little difficult in the beginning, but it's not impossible. Set a little reward for each day you are successful in completing this task. If you quit before the end of seven days, you have two options: accept that you are a complainer with no real plans to improve your life, or push past the uneasy feelings and frustrations that may arise, and keep trying until you succeed.

I always ask my clients what their level of commitment to change is, and it is important that you discover your own answers. Ask yourself: How committed are you? Are you willing to work tenaciously, have an open mind, and push past discomfort to improve your mood? Can you commit to completing everything you say you will do for at least seven days? Will you give up if the results are not instant? Will you not even start because you have no motivation? Will you quit because there is comfort in discomfort? If you can't commit to doing the work or staying motivated, then don't say you'll do it.

DON'T LET SOMEONE ELSE'S MESS AFFECT YOUR HAPPINESS

Many of us spend our time with unhappy, miserable, lost souls. Expecting to attain happiness while being in the company of those who are not happy is akin to hanging around broke people and expecting to learn how to get rich. It just doesn't make sense. Once you learn how to be happy, you will not be able to tolerate people, conditions, or events that make you feel anything less than happy. Life becomes easier when you realize this, and you are better equipped to respond to its ups and downs. A happy person, full of self-love, is a far better partner, child, sibling, employee, friend, and overall person than one who is dog-tired, worn-out, sad, depressed, and anxious. So it is in your best interest to surround yourself with people who have accomplished what you are trying to accomplish, which is to discover happiness.

However, you must be extremely careful with the people you choose to guide you on your road to happiness. It is wise to seek guidance from individuals who are actually happy and whose happiness comes from positivity. There are individuals who find happiness in the misery of others, and these are the people you should staunchly avoid. Seek someone who makes smart decisions, not individuals who talk about being wise but let their lives remain a mess. It makes sense to look to individuals who possess integrity and have the ability to think logically and critically. If they have actually accomplished something you admire, they should be able to give some advice to make your road less bumpy. Most importantly, seek advice from someone who wants you to succeed.

At times, it seems that those closest to us offer the least support. In fact, they can go out of their way to try to set up roadblocks and obstacles in our lives. It's extremely painful to find that the most poisonous venom comes from the mouths of friends and family. Understand that, oftentimes, your family members and friends cannot think outside of their own perspectives for themselves, let alone you. When they are so wrapped up in their own lives and issues, it is hard for them to care for you in the way you might want. Be careful who you share your thoughts and ideas with, because some people are waiting for the opportunity to belittle you because of their own insecurities and shortcomings. It's easy to internalize what they say because they're your loved ones, but you must realize that their comments and actions reflect more on them than you. While it is important to acknowledge that they have hurt you, it is more important to move on from the pain instead of wallowing in it.

The reality is that happy individuals have encountered the same life struggles as everyone else, but they understand that they have a choice in how they perceive, process, and respond to the struggles. Perhaps the biggest difference between happy and unhappy people is that happy individuals take responsibility for their lives and actions and direct their energy where they want their lives to go, instead of letting life just happen to them. Do you take responsibility for your actions? Are you living your life, or is life living you?

A perfect example of this happiness phenomenon is entertainer Tina Turner. I admire very few people, especially celebrities, but I admire her. She suffered years of domestic violence, and when she finally decided she had had enough, her life did a 180. She has not looked back since. Ms.

Turner did not allow herself to become bitter from her abuse. Instead, she garnered the strength to leave everything behind, picked up the pieces, focused on her higher power and talent, and moved on with her life. For years, the focus of interviews always turned to the abuse she suffered. It was clear that Tina worked overtime to maintain composure during this line of questioning, and I know she was thinking, "Why do people keep asking me about this crap?" But she never lashed out. She responded with, "That part of my life is over, and I really don't see a need to keep talking about it." She focused on her future and where her life was going, not where she had been.

You will not find happy people begging or waiting on anyone or anything in order to live fulfilling, purposeful lives. They accept reality, love themselves just as they are, and are true to themselves and their values, regardless of the situation. Typically, happy people make the best of what they have right now instead of whining, "If only this or that would happen." In short, they make the best out of the cards they have been dealt. What have you done with your cards?

Happy individuals are also characterized by adventure, respect, openness, flexibility, and setting good boundaries to maintain their status. If something is in the way of a happy person's goals, they don't deal with it. You will not observe happy people dwelling on the negative. If they do, it is only momentarily. They focus on the positive and grow, even in bad situations. Challenges are viewed as lessons, and growth and strength are the result of overcoming adversity instead of being defeated by it. Positive individuals are bigger than their problems. Are you growing beyond your problems, or are you just repeating them?

Surround yourself with people who are happy. Your mood will change when you are around happy people. If human beings are emotional sponges, whose attitude do you want to soak up: someone who wallows in self-pity and sadness, or someone who knows how to rise above the bad moments and keep smiling? Obviously, you want the latter. When you find your happiness crew, ask what their secrets to a happy life are. What are their approaches to life? How do they maintain their positive mindsets? You will no doubt pick up some invaluable techniques.

DEAL WITH REALITY

Reality is painful, and some people would rather live in a world of denial than deal with reality. Usually, denial is not an effective way to deal with depression and anxiety, but I had one client that denial worked quite well for. He was overwhelmed, dealing with his depression and getting the run around while waiting for a liver transplant. When there was nothing he could do regarding his health situation, he denied the fact that his problems existed to prevent himself from getting worked up and overwhelmed.

I had a client who kept saying her husband had an emotional affair, meaning there was no sex involved. This is what she needed to believe to be okay. Neither Stevie Wonder nor Ray Charles could miss all the physical signs she shared in therapy that pointed to her husband having a sexual affair. This client's previous husband had an affair, and she said it would devastate her if her husband cheated on her. I worked with a gentleman who was in a financial mess because his wife did not pay the bills on time, or at all, and kept getting title loans. He and his wife were facing eviction, the utilities were in arrears, and they were deep in credit card debt, yet he kept expecting his wife to be financially responsible. He just kept saying, "If she does this one more time, I'm leaving."

Taking care of yourself is the foundation to building a solid ground. Some people enjoy being depressed and anxious; I know it sounds crazy, but it's true. There are some individuals who, whether consciously or unconsciously, are comfortable with depression and misery. I'm sure we all know someone who is hell-bent on maintaining misery for themselves and others. They thrive on it. For example, I worked with a sixty-year-old woman whom I was called to see because she was crying uncontrollably. Concerned, I wondered what had just happened to this woman to cause her so much pain. With weary, bloodshot eyes, she cried that her husband left her for another woman. While this was true, he left her twenty years ago. Angrily, she wondered how he had the audacity to bring this woman, who was now his wife, to their daughter's wedding. I spoke with her daughter who said that her mother has been crying over this for twenty years. Ultimately, there was nothing I could do for her while she was adamant on maintaining her suffering and agony. Do you have any long-kept misery that you feel it's time to let go of?

Changing ourselves, a job, relationships or whatever is scary even if it is a desired choice and the outcome is favorable. I understand that it's hard. Uncertainty is a bitch. Feelings of doubt and uncertainty seem to always arise, no matter how confident you are or how positive the outlook is. When change seems imminent, you start to question yourself and consider just staying where you are because it is comfortable and familiar. This is the easy way, and it will leave you stagnant, miserable, and unhappy. You must push past these uneasy feelings and move forward steadfastly with a commitment to succeed. Are you willing to push through any discomfort?

I have observed clients who come to therapy expecting the therapist to tell them what they should or should not do. I have had clients cry, "Tell me what to do," or they'll say, "What would you do?" The problem with this is two-fold. If a therapist tells you what to do and it does not work, it gives you the freedom to blame the therapist instead of taking responsibility. Even if you determine their advice to be "right," you've already created a pattern of not thinking for yourself. So what happens the next time you face an issue? You run back to the therapist because you have not learned to think or problem-solve for yourself. You become dependent on the input of others, which is not the goal of therapy at all. The true goal is to learn how to work on yourself.

A thousand times, I have heard clients chirp, "I don't have any time to work on myself," but these same clients will spend an enormous amount of time and energy on unproductive efforts, like trying to change someone else. I have worked with couples who wasted a lot of energy adamantly stating how their partners need to change, and they aren't the only culprits. Parents try to change their children, children try to change their parents, friends try to change each other, and so forth. We're all guilty of this.

There is only one person you have the power to change, and that is you. Keeping your own wig on straight is more than enough work, and you'll go crazy trying to change someone else. If you had the power to change others, you probably would not be reading this book or in therapy. What you can change is how you perceive, process, and respond to life's events or situations. Honestly, what even gives you the right to tell others how they should think and feel and what they should do? Unless they have asked for your advice explicitly, it's not your place. Everyone has freedom of choice, good or bad. Just because someone's choices are not identical to yours does not necessarily make them wrong or make them a bad person. So if you find yourself entrenched in the life of someone whose choices you do not like, then you have some decisions of your own to make. You can only change yourself, which is hard enough without trying to work on someone else's mess as well. And as for the "lack of time" excuse, if you break your butt to watch *Scandal* and *Empire*, spend inordinate amounts of time on Facebook, Instagram, and Twitter, and constantly play games like Candy Crush, you have more than enough time to work on yourself.

Something magical happens when we work on ourselves. Answers and solutions to problems and concerns become crystal clear. Your ability to think through situations and events with a balance of emotions, logic, and common sense increases. As you change your mindset and how you perceive, process, and respond to life's experiences, you respond differently, and life becomes easier and lighter.

CONCLUSION

I have come to the conclusion that people really do not want to feel. Rather than feel, and deal with our emotions, we want to pop a pill, resort to drugs and alcohol, gamble our money away, shop until we drop, remain in empty relationships, use other unproductive forms of coping, and retreat back to being comfortable in discomfort. We are humans, not Vulcanites from Star Trek. We are supposed to feel emotions. If something unpleasant happens, you are supposed to feel sad. If you are meeting someone for the first time, it is expected that one would feel anxious. Humans are supposed to feel emotions.

Life consists of joy and pain, ups and downs, and experiences we like and dislike. The positive experiences are, of course, a welcome pleasure; but dealing with the negative is what some people want to run from. To deal with problems, we may ignore them, to avoid sadness and pain. Sometimes, we feel they are simply too much to overcome, and, to cope, we employ bad habits that only help on a short-term basis. In fact, most of the popular coping methods, like drug use, excessive shopping, gambling, and eating disorders, eventually lead to more depression and anxiety. Depression, anxiety, feelings of being overwhelmed, and stress are alarm systems of the mind and body. They are meant to tell you that something is not right or is out of balance. Ignoring those alarms just makes matters worse.

Learn to become bigger than your problems. Stop letting fear be an obstacle. Stop permitting the slightest little stumbling block to cause you to retreat and give up. Fear should not stop you from completing anything you set your mind on accomplishing. Veteran performers, whether in show business or sports, admit to fear before each performance. However, the show goes on in spite of fear, and things usually turn out well. Quit thinking that you have to get rid of fear, doubt, and worry before you can get into action. Act in spite of fear, uncertainty, and discomfort. You can have struggles and trials in life and can still live a life of happiness, filled with joy and peace.

Every single person I have worked with who overcame depression and anxiety did so because they made a decision that enough was enough and took action to acquire the life they wanted. All the therapy techniques, books, CDs, videos, and lectures of T.D. Jakes, Charles Stanley, Andy Stanley, Wayne Dyer, Les Brown, Joel Osteen, Dr. Phil McGraw, Steve Harvey, Wallace Wattle, David Henry Thoreau, and Dale Carnegie, who are some of my personal favorites, or even my own guidance cannot help you if you have not made a decision and a commitment to changing your life. At some point, you have to stop talking about being happy and start taking steps to be happy. Without action, the advice given will amount to nothing more than ineffective words, and you'll likely find that acquiring health, happiness, and peace, or whatever you desire, will most likely remain an elusive dream.

Steve Salerno, author of *Sham: How the Self-Help Movement Made America Helpless,* states that market research shows that customers who purchase self-help products, such as books and tapes, will purchase another self-help product within 18 months of their first purchase. Salerno goes as far as to call the self-help industry exploitive. I disagree. Was the book or tape purchase a waste of time, or did the reader not apply any of the suggestions?

Life is about choices. A common complaint of those with depression and anxiety is, "I can't get out of bed." But if the house caught fire, you would surely get out of bed and do so quickly. So it is not that you cannot overcome your depression and anxiety, but it's up to you to make a choice not to get out of bed and blame it on depression. Depression and anxiety may make it hard to get out of bed, but getting out of bed is possible if you choose to do it. Getting out of depression and anxiety is a choice.

Recently, a client summed up overcoming depression and anxiety quite nicely. He reflected on his personal experience and remarked, "If you control your thoughts, you control your happiness. Try to look at the glass as half full. You can think yourself into bad thoughts, but you don't have to be at the mercy of your emotions." He concluded, "I can control my depression. I can implement the techniques learned, or keep going down the same old path. In order to maintain my sanity, I need to stop – take a breather, apply the techniques, and control my destiny and ultimately live a happy life."

"Most of the people who died yesterday had plans for today. Better start appreciating every day God gives you." – FeFe 87

References

America's startling' use of mental-illness drugs: Understanding why Americans are taking more pills to treat mental illness. The Week. November 18, 2011.

Any Anxiety Disorder Among Adults. National Institute of Mental Health website. Update October 2015.

Brown, L. (1992). Live Your Dreams. New York: Harper Collins.

Burns, D. D. (1980). *Feeling Good: The New Mood Therapy* (preface by Aaron T. Beck). New York: Wm. Morrow and Co (hardbound); New American Library, 1981 (paperback). Revised and updated, 1999.

Burns, D. D. (2006). *When Panic Attacks.* New York: Morgan Road Books.

Carnegie, D. (1984). How to Stop Worrying and Start Living. New York: Simon & Schuster.

De Jong, P., Kim Berg, I. (2013). Interviewing for Solutions. Brooks/Cole: Belmont.

The Economic Burden of Anxiety Disorders, a study commissioned by ADAA (The Journal of Clinical Psychiatry, 60(7), July 1999).

King, K. (2012). Power of the Pussy How to Get What You Want From Men: Love, Respect, Commitment and More!: Dating and Relationship Advice for Women. Amazon.

Luskin, F. August 30, 2012. Forgiveness, Stress Management, and Happiness: Dr. Luskin (http://www.inflection.com.

McGraw, P. (2009). Life Code – The New Rules for Winning in the Real World. Bird Street Books: Los Angeles.

Olff, M., Frijling, J., Kubzansky, L., Bradley, B. Ellenbogen, M., Cardoso, C., Bartz, J., Yee, J., van Zuiden, M. The role of oxytocin in social bonding, stress regulation and mental health: An update on the moderating effects of context and interindividual differences.

Psychoneuroendocrinology. Volume 38, Issue 9, September 2013, Pages 1883–1894.

Salerno, S. (2005). *Sham: How the Self-Help Movement Made America Helpless*. "Whatever they think you're deficient in, they're selling the solution." Random House: New York.

Turner, T., Loder, K. (1987). I Tina. Harper Collins: New York.

Wattles, W. (1911). The Science of Getting Rich. Elizabeth Towne: Massachusetts.

Made in the USA
Charleston, SC
06 May 2016